River Series
RE-ORDER
Niger Manilla
No.2004

The Origins of Form in Art

THE ORIGINS OF FORM IN ART

HERBERT READ

LONDON
THAMES AND HUDSON

1003446073

Contents

Preface

This volume is further evidence of my constant search for a social, indeed, a biological principle in art. Art has many functions, most of them sufficiently obvious and delightful. Its persistence as a communal activity from the time of the earliest records of civilization to our own disordered age would seem to indicate an essential role in human development. That such a role is not merely representational, but is active in the deepest sources of cognition, has been evident to every great philosopher from Plato to Cassirer. Art is the ability given to man to separate a form from the swirling chaos of his sensations, and to contemplate that form in its uniqueness. But how did such an ability arise? At what moment in the evolution of human consciousness did form by some mysterious alchemy emerge from perceptual indifference or indeterminacy? Henri Focillon, who alone has ventured into this field of essential aesthetics, has suggested that life itself is a creator of forms, and there is indeed no distinction between life and art in this matter. 'Life is form, and form is the modality of life. The relationships that bind forms together in nature cannot be pure chance, and what we call "natural life" is in effect a relationship between forms, so inexorable that without it this natural life could not exist. So it is with art as well. The formal relationships within a work of art and among different works of art constitute an order for, and a metaphor of, the entire universe.'[1]

My formulation of this truth will not be so metaphorical, nor so eloquent, as Focillon's, but I think my purpose is the same – to identify art with the life force itself, in so far as this force achieves, in human consciousness, the establishment of being. This last phrase is reminiscent of Heidegger's metaphysics, as well it might be, for he too, in so far as I am able to understand his difficult thought, would ascribe this same function to art.

In general, the intention of these and other writers on the subject (I might have mentioned Conrad Fiedler and Wilhelm Worringer, but their names will crop up from time to time in my text) is to redeem art from the secondary and indeed trivial role ascribed to it by traditional philosophy and to make it the primary instrument of our cognition of reality.

Some of these essays are indebted indirectly to the work of two colleagues (who are also my friends). The first is Lancelot Law Whyte, a physicist, who has maintained in a series of books and lectures, that *nature is essentially formative* – that one 'unitary principle' or 'ordering tendency' is manifested in physics, biology and psychology. Mr Whyte would extend the same principle to the sphere of art, aesthetic discrimination being the first conscious manifestation of the unitary principle in human artifacts.

The second colleague is a student of art with an exceptional knowledge of psycho-analysis, Adrian Stokes. In five related books published within the past decade Mr Stokes, applying the psycho-analytical doctrines of Melanie Klein, has demonstrated that the search for coherence or clarity of form is the basic drive in artistic creation, and that this drive is an unconscious attempt to restore or reconstitute the harmonious unity of the primary mother-child relationship. This is a very simplified statement of a somewhat complex theory, for what is reconstituted is not so much an emotional bond as the sensuous apprehension of what is called the whole-object, the whole-object being an unconscious memory of the mother's breast.

My own approach, it will be seen, is more eclectic, but the evidence proceeding from these two quite diverse directions should be added to my own distinct approach to the subject.

Most of the essays collected here have had previous publication in various journals, as indicated in the footnote on the first page of each essay. I would like to express my gratitude to the editors of these journals for the hospitality of their pages. I would also like to thank the Trustees of the Center for Advanced Studies at Wesleyan University (Middletown, Connecticut) for giving me the opportunity, during the tenure of a Fellowship at that Center, of writing some of these essays and revising the rest.

H.R.

December, 1964

I

Originality

Originality is not the urge to be different from others, to produce
the brand-new; it is to grasp (in the etymological sense) the
origin, the roots of both ourselves and things. MAX RAPHAEL

'There is nothing new under the sun' – how often we hear that
saying, uttered perhaps to console those who have no gift for
discovery, or more likely to discourage the search for truths that
might upset our complacency. So acceptable is the saying that
Sir Thomas Browne did not include it among his *Pseudodoxia
Epidemica or Vulgar Errors*, nor Charles Lamb among his *Popular
Fallacies*. From antiquity to our own time it has been the habit of
philosophers and moralists to frown on innovation – on innovation in religion or in art. It is only in science and technology
that innovation, or invention, has been recognized as a principle
of life itself.

And yet an unconscious desire for novelty is one of the strongest
impulses in the average man or woman: a desire for new fashions
in clothes or furnishings; for strange food and exotic scenery;
and is not the instinct of procreation the expression of a desire
for the most original of all things, a new human being, a recognizable member of the species, but not, we pray, a duplicate of
ourselves or of anyone else?

Sewanee Review, LXI, 1953.

In this book I shall be concerned mostly with the problem of originality in art, but the biological analogy is not irrelevant. The main drive in animal evolution, we are told, is the desire of the species to reproduce itself, and though under the influence of natural selection a species may divide up into sub-species, and thus differentiate itself from itself, the process is explained by material factors: the difference in kind resolves into an immense but calculable number of differences in degree. Here there is no originality in our sense of the word, but a chain of material cause and effect to which we give the name 'natural selection'. But in addition to natural selection, the science of evolution has detected the occasional occurrence of 'sports' or chance mutations, and these sometimes lead to the birth of what the American biologist Goldschmidt has called a 'hopeful monster',[1] a sport not subject to prediction or calculation, a new thing newly created, which in a favourable environment may succeed in establishing itself. But I must not press this analogy, for the hopeful monster of evolution is not only a very rare animal, but sometimes degenerate or recessive.

Originality in mental evolution – and particularly in the mental history of an individual – has far more significance than this analogy would suggest. The main usefulness of the biological evidence is to show that originality as a phenomenon is not unnatural, not outside the nature of things.

It is time to give a preliminary definition of what we mean by originality in mental processes – and particularly of what is meant by originality in art. Is originality a general quality that can be isolated for definition, or is it rather an unpredictable event which we may hope for but cannot invoke?

To answer such questions adequately would involve a long excursion into psychology, and particularly into the psychology of the artist. Instead of that, I shall resort to one or two metaphors, in the belief that they will convey my meaning more effectively than a scientific analysis. Perhaps only one metaphor is involved, but I shall compare its use by a Chinese poet of the fourth century, and by a Swiss painter of the twentieth century. The Chinese poet is Lu Chi, who wrote a prose poem on the Art of Letters, the *Wen Fu*, which has been translated with a commentary by Professor E. R. Hughes.[2] It is a fascinating document, only fifteen pages long in the English translation, but of a clarity and concentration that puts modern learning to shame. I do not think that western psychology has added anything of value to the explanation it gives of the artistic process.

Towards the end of his poem Lu Chi comes to the problem of inspiration, and I will quote the paragraph as translated by Professor Hughes:

1. As to the interaction of stimulus and response, the intermingling of the flow with the blocking of the flow:
2. their coming cannot be prevented,
   their going cannot be stopped:
3. underground things go on like shadows vanishing, back to life they come like echoes awakening.
4. Comes the lightening release of nature's spring – where, then, is disorder and unreason?
5. The wind of thought comes forth from the breast, a fountain of words is in the teeth and the lips:
6. A riot of tender shoots thrusting up in mixed abundance – which brush and silk alone can discriminate:[3]
7. a pattern emblazoned to fill the eye, a music remote yet flooding the ear.

Here the image is that of a two-way process, an ebb and flow over whose alternation the poet or painter has no control. The source is underground, in the unconscious, and the flow is released, not by the will, but by Nature – that is to say, by the attainment of a certain degree of readiness, attention, or maturity. There is a treatise on the Japanese art of archery[4] which goes into this point in great detail, maintaining that the most difficult achievement in shooting with the bow is just this waiting for the natural release of the string: a moment that comes with serenity and detachment, with an utter absence of striving. The flow of inspiration begins in exactly the same way, and brings with it, as Lu Chi says, a fountain of words, which the poet suddenly finds in the teeth and the lips. Now comes the final and perhaps the most important stage in the artistic process: the poet must discriminate among this mixed abundance, that is to say, make a pattern that is pleasing to the senses – images that fill the eye, music that floods the ear – and he does this with the instruments of his craft – with brush on silk, or as we should say, with pen on paper. Skill is necessary at this stage – what Lu Chi calls 'the rules of diction and the musical patterning in writing'.

In Paul Klee's almost equally short and equally pregnant treatise on modern art,[5] we find a similar image – the creation of a work of art is compared to the growth of a tree, which has its roots in the earth, its crown in the air. From the outspreading roots of the tree the sap flows to the artist, who stands as the trunk of the tree, and out of the fulness of this flow he moulds his vision which unfolds and spreads as the crown of the tree. Again the image of a flow, a flow which alternates with the seasons, without conscious effort, but in Klee's image we have the additional idea of transformation – the idea that art is not a mirrored reflection of a given reality, but the transformation of one element (which has its roots underground, in the unconscious) into another element (made conscious in time and space). The artist is merely a channel whose only function is to transmit the forces of nature into the forms of art.

Klee's metaphor is much the same as Lu Chi's, and at first sight it would seem that neither metaphor leaves much room for anything that might be called originality. In both metaphors the role of the artist seems to be passive – a channel or conduit through which forces flow from one realm of reality to another realm of reality – in psychological terms, from the unconscious to the conscious. Now this is perhaps the subtlest point to be seized in our argument – I mean the difference between an event for which the artist is consciously responsible, and an event in which the artist is a passive instrument. We do not credit the midwife with the creation of the child she brings into the world: is there any more reason for crediting the artist with the creation of the work of art he spontaneously delivers: with the generation of the wind of thought that comes forth from the breast?

Our metaphors are in danger of getting a little mixed, for the artist is his own midwife. But has he conceived the child he brings forth? According to Lu Chi and Klee, no! 'His position is humble', says Klee. 'And the beauty of the crown is not his own. He is merely a channel.' 'This thing which is in me', cries Lu Chi, 'but which no efforts of mine can slay!' – 'The this-thing's-in-me-ness' is the literal rendering, according to Professor Hughes. 'Wherefore time and again I stroke my empty bosom in pity for myself: so ignorant am I of what causes the opening and the barring of the door.' I think that both Lu Chi and Klee assume that what comes out of the unconscious has never been seen before, and in that sense is original; but that does not correspond with our modern idea of the unconscious as a repository of suppressed instincts and experiences, both individual and collect-ive. And there still is the possibility, at any rate in Lu Chi's account of the artistic process, that originality occurs in the conscious treatment of the material released from the unconscious – in the process of discrimination and judgment, the 'patterning' of the material. But subject to these provisos, which will be taken up in the further course of our argument, we seem to be arriving at a preliminary definition of originality, which while admitting the phenomenon, as a concrete object or explicit event, refuses to give the individual artist any credit for it, except perhaps a certain obstetric skill. That, of course, is not the accepted sense of the term, for in modern usage originality is regarded as a unique gift, a capacity possessed by a very special kind of person.

This modern conception of originality begins with the Romantic Movement. Goethe and Schelling, Kierkegaard and Coleridge, would often speak of the spontaneous nature of any apprehension of truth, and more particularly of the spontaneous nature of any act of creation in the fine arts. Spontaneity in itself is not, of course, a guarantee of originality, as I have just observed: we have only to consider the spasmodic operations of memory, which is the recovery of precisely what is not original, to realize that we must seek for some other distinguishing quality. I have also, and for the same reason, dismissed the unconscious as a source of originality: not only is the unconscious, as the psychoanalysts define it, a reservoir of past and forgotten experiences, but art and thought, in so far as they are original, are products of conscious processes. As Vivante[6] says, 'art, far from being nonconscious, is a conquest of consciousness [a "discrimination", as Lu Chi said]. Wherever we enter the realm of art our obscure impressions become intelligible, and their becoming intelligible belongs to the essence of artistic creation.' For all their interests and stimulus, those forms of modern art which have relied on the automatic projection of dreams and phantasies are not in the proper sense of the words either creative or original. I am not condemning, as will become evident as I proceed, all those works of art that were produced, between the wars, as manifestations of superrealism – on the contrary, I think that by now we should be in a position to distinguish between what is boring because it was automatic and uninhibited, and what is still interesting because it was an original revelation. Admittedly, the artists themselves did not always know when they were engaged on a conquest of conciousness, and when they were merely exploiting the unconscious, or rather, letting loose 'the riot of tender shoots'. In the early paintings of Chirico, for example, and generally in Paul Klee's work, we are made conscious of 'a pattern emblazoned to fill the eye'; I do not find the same positive value in the arbitrary fantasies of Salvador Dali.

Let us define originality as a phenomenon which did not exist before a specific moment of time, and which is, at that moment brought into existence, 'developed' in the mind as image or event. Whether the reaction of which we become conscious is material or immaterial, plastic or conceptual, a work of art or an observation, does not matter at present. But we must elucidate our notion of 'bringing into existence'. This means more than the creation, in one or more people, of a state of awareness. We can be aware, in some numinous or intuitive sense, of the realm of essences – ideas, qualities, attributes which

1. *Jean Dubuffet.   The Cow with the Glad Eye.   1954*

2. Paul Klee. *Death and Fire.* 1940

are too universal to be localized. They are 'intangible', but not inconceivable. What is necessary, to constitute originality, is the conversion of the notional essence into some concrete and factual material – into words, for example; or into shapes of wood or stone, into areas of colour or vibrations of sound. Thought can be original – it always is, argues Vivante, if it is concerned with realities, for the reality of words is essentially the reality of life. We establish, or have established through long periods of time, our sense of reality by creating, for each clarified and detachable experience, a clear and appropriate symbol – vocal sounds which were eventually stabilized as words. Every word was once an original work of art, or part of a complex vocal structure that was an original work of art. We still, though rarely, create original words, though none with the magical intensity given to them by our primitive ancestors. A poet nevertheless remains one who can use words with a magical function, generally by combining them in such a manner that they serve as descriptive symbols for new insights, new emotions, wider areas of consciousness. It is in this sense that Hölderlin described poetry as 'establishment', as the giving of reality and substance to human insights and emotions by the act of *naming*. 'That which remains, is established by the poets.'[8]

The poet may be a coiner of new words – Shakespeare added several new words to the language, and Coleridge even more; but what the poet invents is more often a new meaning. He changes the meaning of an existing word, or creates a new meaning by an unusual combination of words. And there, as Owen Barfield has said, 'is one of the exact points at which the genius, the *originality*, of the individual poet has first entered the world'. I quote further from this unduly neglected critic:

'The objection will possibly be raised that this dwelling upon the meanings of individual words is a precious and dilettante kind of criticism. But, as a matter of fact (sententious as it must sound) the reverse is the truth. Words whose meanings are relatively fixed and established, words which can be

defined – words, that is, which are used with precisely the
same connotation by different speakers – are *results*, they are *things
become*. The arrangement and re-arrangement of such unequivocal
terms in a series of propositions is the function of *logic*, whose
object is elucidation, and the elimination of error. The poetic has
nothing to do with this. It can only manifest itself as *fresh meaning;*
it operates essentially *within* the individual term, which it creates
and re-creates by the magic of new combinations. . . . Thus, the
poet's relation to terms is that of maker. And it is in this making
of terms – whether the results are to be durable or fleeting – that
we can divine the very poetic itself.'[9]

The whole of my argument might be conducted at this linguistic
level, if only we could rely on the common possession of a lively
sense of the magical function of words in poetry. But no material
used for creative purposes by mankind has become so debased
as language – it is now a dull mass from which poetry can be
distilled only by somewhat complicated processes. Poetry, indeed,
now relies to a considerable extent on what might be called visual
potency: it is the electrical discharge which takes place when two
or more opposed but related images are brought into proximity:

> Rat's coat, crowskin, crossed staves
> In a field
> Behaving as the wind behaves . . .

The magic is evoked by the images the words signify, and is not
wholly conveyed by the words themselves. Words such as 'crow-
skin' are as original as a word can be in our time – that is to say,
they are unfamiliar. But originally every word was original: used
for the first time and adopted by a community of human beings as
a magical symbol. A foreign language can still be magical to us,
as when we listen to a poem or an opera in an unknown tongue.
The Vulgate, as used in religious rites, must still have some of
this magical appeal, though, and perhaps because, the meaning
of the words is only vaguely apprehended, or perhaps because
the meaning is not to be apprehended by a cursory reading. A
modern European, Owen Barfield points out, 'can read Plato and

Aristotle through from end to end, he can even write books expounding their philosophy, and all without understanding a single sentence. Unless he has enough imagination, and enough power of detachment from the established meanings or thought-forms of his own civilization, to enable him to grasp the meanings of fundamental terms – unless, in fact, he has the power not only of thinking, but of *un-thinking* – he will simply reinterpret everything they say in terms of subsequent thought. If he merely seeks to deduce the meaning of terms like *arche*, *logos*, *psyche*, *dynamis*, etc., from the general context, if he cannot rather *feel* the way in which they *came into being out of the essential nature of the Greek consciousness as a whole*, he may read pages and pages of Greek letterpress, and enjoy them, but he will know no more than the shadow of Greek meaning.'[10]

When we first begin to appreciate the quality of foreign poetry, Greek and Latin poetry especially, the words have a magical quality, though we may call it something else. Matthew Arnold spoke of the 'nobleness' of Homer's language, of 'a perfect lovely grandeur'; his poetry has, he said, 'the pure lines of an Ionian horizon, the liquid clearness of an Ionian sky'. Words do not evoke such metaphors because of their logical connotations, but because they are used with freshness, that is to say, as though minted for the first time, originally. And that, too, is Shakespeare's great quality: the impression he gives of using words for the first time, or at any rate, for the first time in a particular context. That is, as we say, his originality.

> In such a night as this,
> When the sweet wind did gently kiss the trees
> And they did make no noise,–
> In such a night
> Stood Dido with a willow in her hand
> Upon the wild sea banks, and waft her love
> To come again to Carthage,–

The words in such a passage are simple, for the most part mono-syllabic, and only 'Dido' and 'Carthage' introduce an exotic note.

The originality, Shakespeare's originality, lies in the musical combination of these common sounds – in the subtle play with alliteration, with vowel correspondences, with consonantal echoes – we can analyse the magic, and label its constituents with our harsh technical terms, but we do not thereby explain the act of discrimination or judgment that brought these words into this particular combination. That cannot be explained by any analytical procedure, by any appeal to tradition or training: the secret belongs to the unique make of Shakespeare's personality: to his absolute sense of appropriate form.

Consider, for a moment, the opposite quality that words can have – their staleness, their 'hackneyed' or tired effect. We then call them 'clichés' – that is to say, words from a stamp, stereotyped words, duplicate words, words lacking precisely the quality of uniqueness or originality.

The greatest enemy of originality is, perhaps, the *Zeitgeist*, that pervasive spirit in a country which at a particular period of time unconsciously compels artists of all kinds to adopt a common idiom, to relinquish their personal choice of language. We are familiar nowadays, for example, with the following kind of verse:

> Out of this, out of the first incision
> Of mortality on mortality, there comes
> The genuflexion, and the partition of pain
> Between man and God; there grows the mutual
>   action,
> The perspective of the vision.
> Out of this, out of the dereliction
> Of a mild morning, comes the morning's motive,
> The first conception, the fusion of root and sky;
> Grows the achievement of the falling shadow,
> Pain's patient benediction.

That comes from a play by Christopher Fry [11], but you might have guessed, not unreasonably, that it came from a play by T. S. Eliot. Mr Eliot arrived on the scene first with this particular idiom, but even so I do not find anything very personal in it (Mr Eliot's personality expresses itself in another kind of idiom, of which I have already given an example). But the *Zeitgeist* is usually more insidious than this, and we do not recognize its voice until we get a long way from it. We cannot now read with any pleasure the once popular verse of Bowles or Rogers, and little enough of Campbell or Moore, or of Southey or Hunt; but in their time (which was the time of Wordsworth and Coleridge, of Shelley and Keats), they seemed to be the typical, the *influential* verse of the time. 'The reader', wrote Coleridge in his disillusioned days, 'must make himself acquainted with the general style of composition that was at that time deemed poetry, in order to understand and account for the effect produced on me by the *Sonnets*, the *Monody at Matlock*, and the *Hope*, of Mr Bowles; for it is peculiar to original genius to become less and less *striking*, in proportion to its success in improving the taste and judgement of its contemporaries.'[12] We read the Sonnets of Bowles today, and wonder what could ever have been 'striking' about them; and if Bowles struck his contemporaries as 'original', originality is something different from what we had supposed.

Is originality, then, merely a contrast to the typical style of any period, itself destined to sink to the level of the commonplace as it becomes acceptable to a wider public? That might be an acceptable generalization if there were not this difference between the genius that retains its brightness, as Shakespeare's genius has done, and the genius that simply fades away, as the genius that Coleridge found in Bowles has done. But we need not compare Bowles with Shakespeare: there is Coleridge himself, his disciple. What did the disciple discover that the master did not hand down to him?

There is plenty in Coleridge's verse, both in sentiment and in expression, that does not rise more than a measurable degree above Bowles. Then suddenly, for the space of two or three brief years, his wings are spread and he touches the heights of Parnassus – he writes the *Rime of the Ancient Mariner*, *Christabel*, *Kubla Khan*. Did Coleridge momentarily become more intelligent, more proficient in the technique of verse, a more dutiful follower of the tradition of English poetry? Obviously not. He was visited by a poetic afflatus, an inspired state of mind in which the words came as come they must, 'in which all the images rose up before him as *things*, with a parallel production of the correspondent expressions, without any sensation or consciousness of effort'. Such is the state of inspiration – 'the lightening release of Nature's spring' – and such is the state of origination; but it is not everything, as Coleridge discovered. He was interrupted by a person from Porlock and when he returned to his pen and paper his flow had been blocked. He could not recover the inspiration.

At this linguistic level the existence of originality is obvious. What, then, is the case against originality? I shall examine two discussions of the process of creation, one in the sphere of poetry, the other in the sphere of painting. It will be found that they both agree in substituting for the notion of originality the notion of development, or tradition – that is to say, the notion of an evolution uninterrupted by mutation, the notion of a conscious control of the process of creation.

I shall first take the point of view presented by a poet whose own work I have used to illustrate my theme: T.S.Eliot; it occurs in his Introduction to the *Selected Poems* of Ezra Pound.[13] This is not the only place in which Eliot discusses the question: indeed, it might be said that all his criticism centres round the relationship between 'Tradition and the Individual Talent', to repeat the title of an essay in which he first stated the problem. But in that essay he had merely to deal with generalities. In the case of Pound he was faced with the task of defending, or justifying, a poet whose work he greatly admired, but a poet indicted under the charges of modernity, eccentricity, and licence – in one word, originality. How was a reconciliation to be effected?

Well, first by a countercharge. 'Pound's versification is objectionable to those who object to it as "modern", because they have not sufficient education (in verse) to understand development.' Pound's modernity, that is to say, is an illusion, or at least, a misunderstanding. But let us see how Eliot develops his argument.

'Poets may be divided', he says, 'into those who develop technique, those who imitate technique, and those who invent technique. When I say "invent" [continues Eliot], I should use inverted commas, for invention would be irreproachable if it were possible. "Invention" is wrong only because it is impossible. I mean that the difference between the "development" and the "sport" is, in poetry, a capital one. There are two kinds of "sports" in poetry, in the floricultural sense. One is the imitation of development, and the other is the imitation of some idea of originality. The former is commonplace, a waste product of civilization, the latter is contrary to life.'

I pause there to point out that Eliot does not seem to have heard of the evolutionary scientist's 'hopeful monster'. If there are hopeful monsters in life, may they not also exist in literature?

Eliot continues: 'The poem which is absolutely original is absolutely bad; it is, in the bad sense, "subjective", with no relation to the world to which it appeals.

'Originality, in other words, is by no means a simple idea in the criticism of poetry. True originality is merely development; and if it is right development it may appear in the end so *inevitable* that we almost come to the point of view of denying all "original" virtue to the poet. He simply did the next thing.'

I detect some equivocation in the use of the word 'next' here. Either we must assume that T. S. Eliot was a dialectical materialist, to whom every event is a link in a causal chain; or that 'the next thing', though coming immediately after the thing before, is a slightly different thing. But if it is slightly different, it is to that extent original.

Eliot goes on to suggest that 'Pound's originality is genuine in that his versification is a logical development of the verse of his English predecessors'. Again, I must ask is a 'logical' development a deterministic development; or do we admit a more irrational 'symbolic' logic? 'We confound under the same name', says Eliot, 'those who are revolutionary because they develop logically, and those who are "revolutionary" because they innovate illogically.' And he adds: 'It is *very* difficult, at any moment, to discriminate between the two.' It sounds like the distinction the communists draw between the true revolutionary and a 'left' deviationist. Perhaps in essence it is the same distinction, for there is no one who is more 'logical' in his theory of development than an orthodox Marxian.

Eliot concludes his discussion of the question by asserting that 'Pound is often more "original" in the right sense, when he is most "archaeological" in the ordinary sense. . . . One of Pound's most indubitable claims to genuine originality is . . . his revivification of the Provençal and the early Italian poetry. . . . He is much more modern, in my opinion, when he deals with Italy and Provence, than when he deals with modern art. . . . When he deals with antiquities, he extracts the essentially living; when he deals with contemporaries, he sometimes notes only the accidental. . . .'

It will be observed that Eliot has shifted the basis of his argument from technique to subject-matter, from versification to ethics, from an essentially living past to an accidental present. This confirms my view that the opposition to originality in the arts is usually a moral one, or perhaps a political one, and that the moral or political objection gets unconsciously transferred to the artistic method. I would be the last to deny that there is in Pound's verse a large element that is derivative, imitative, and (to me) irritatingly archaic and affected. If I take a poem of Pound's that I admire unreservedly – the 79th Canto, for example – I find traces of Mr Pound's eclectic reading in several languages, but above it all, and subduing it all, compounding it all, if a pun may be allowed, a voice, an accent, a sensibility – that is new in literature, a hopeful monster if ever there was one, and one that is rapidly multiplying its species, especially in America.

Now let me turn to a discussion of originality in the plastic arts: it comes from a writer who will not be suspected of the same moral prejudices as Eliot – M. André Malraux, who has been described as 'novelist, colonel, esthetician, socialist and proud'.[14] In his recent book, *The Psychology of Art*,[15] he has attacked our aesthetic problem with fresh and illuminating energy. In the second volume of this work M. Malraux develops the thesis that art is not the imitation of nature, but of art – art is, as it were, an independent species, mating and spawning in isolation from other species of human activity. It will be seen that there is plenty of scope for the biological analogy in such a thesis. Influences are matched, and a sort of Mendelian law leads by genetic stages to all the recognized varieties of artistic style. A style is defined as 'a means of re-fashioning the world in terms of the values of him who invents it', but 'invention' is not the same as 'origination'. Every artist's career, according to Malraux, begins with a period of apprenticeship, of slavish imitation. 'The fact that it is not some supremely beautiful face which launches the painter on his career, but the sight of a beautiful painting, does not lessen the emotion this experience gives him; and, like all deep emotion, the emotion which springs from art has a craving to perpetuate itself.'

This would fit in well enough with Mr Eliot's conception of tradition, which is predominantly technical: the poet or painter is one who *modifies* the means of expression he inherits from his predecessors, but who does not presume to *invent* new means. You learn the craft of writing, or the craft of painting, just as the carpenter and the bricklayer learn their crafts, and it is only when you have mastered the craft that you venture to do anything original. But what is that something whose creation turns certain craftsmen into artists? M. Malraux provides an answer to that question, which goes further, I think, than Eliot ever ventured. 'I name that man artist', says Malraux, 'who *creates* forms, be he an ambassador like Rubens, an image maker like Gilbert of Autun, an *ignotus* like the Master of Chartres, an illuminator of manuscripts like Limbourg, a court official like Velasquez, a *rentier* like Cézanne, a man possessed like Van Gogh, or a vagabond like Gauguin; I call that man a craftsman who *reproduces* forms, however great may be the charm – or the sleight – of his craftsmanship. . . . Painters and sculptors, whenever they were great, transfigured the forms they had inherited, and the creative joy of him who had *invented* the Moissac *Christ*, the Chartres *Kings*, and the *Uta*, was different in kind from the satisfaction felt by the cabinet-maker who had just completed a perfect chest.'

If I may simplify M. Malraux's thesis, it would seem that in art we have two elements – on the one hand *form*, on the other hand *value*. Forms are normally imitated, copied, handed down from generation to generation by craftsmen. But from time to time along comes a special kind of craftsman, special because he possesses a particular vision of the world, a peculiar way of seeing the world, and this leads to a modification of the traditional forms of expression, to a *transformation*.

Now M. Malraux is not so crude as to assert that the artist 'expresses values', or *wants* to express them. That would lead to the heresy that forms are a logical expression of values, to be determined by the intellect. It is quite obvious that they are often illogical, and that their discovery is accidental. 'Whereas it is the mind that seeks, it is – very often – the hand that finds.' An artist, indeed, is often unconscious of his discovery – it lurks in the background of his canvas; or as M. Malraux says, it is made 'on the side'. It is not intentional, not *willed*. Schiller long ago came to the conclusion that 'the creation of something new is not accomplished by the intellect, but by the play of instinct, from some inner necessity'.[16]

It will be seen that we are thrown back on the individual – on the uniqueness of his mental disposition and the privateness of his experience. But this is where the difficulty arises, for it is not the sense of privateness, or the peculiarity of a personality, that the artist expresses when he is being most original. To take one of M. Malraux's examples, there is no expression of the individual sculptor's personality in the Moissac *Christ*. That happens to be the work of an anonymous artist, but let us transfer the argument to a modern sculptor – Mr Henry Moore. I am well acquainted with Mr Moore's personality, and I am well acquainted with his sculpture. I cannot relate the two, in any sense of expressive equivalence. But I can relate this sculpture to certain specific works of art in the past – a reclining Mexican figure, Michelangelo, a painting by Masaccio – and to certain works of nature – a worn pebble, the shape of a bone, the outline of a mountain range. These are formal entities, and the artist takes a hint from one, and a hint from another, perhaps from many sources, and in that way gets his suggestion of a new form, of a synthetic form. There are degrees of eclecticism, and another artist may find his suggestion in a single source, and that source may be the work of his immediate predecessors. His invention is perhaps only a slight modification of a formal tradition, and it is only when many such modifications have succeeded one another that a change of style becomes obvious – the rise of a style like Mannerism is a good example. But the decisive changes of style are more dramatic, and can generally be attributed to one individual, or to an intimate group or coterie. Again, we have in animal evolution an analogous distinction between micro-mutations and macro-mutations. Macro-mutation is clearly present in the evolution of modern painting, for though this evolution is complex, and has its origins as far back as Constable and Delacroix, yet there are several individual artists whose personal intervention has decisively altered the course of that development. Cézanne and Picasso are the most significant cases – Cézanne, indeed – a hopeful monster if ever there was one – provoked a revolution simply by an innocent concentration on one formal problem: the realization of space by the juxtaposition of areas of pure colour. From his experiments Picasso and Braque seized the notion of a formal analysis of the object: the breakdown of the image of perception into its dominant planes. Juan Gris jumped to the possibility of a *synthesis* of significant planes, representation becoming the secondary purpose of painting. The final outcome of that experiment was an abstract or constructive art, not related to the natural object, but attempting to create an entirely new object, a new reality. Because we are so near to these events we can name the individuals who took a decisive part in them – who gave a *turn* to the events, as we say: a Picasso, a Juan Gris, a Kandinsky, a Klee, a Moore, a Gabo. But the events are explicable without the names: a few hundred pictures in a row, beginning with Cézanne and ending with a Ben Nicholson, would present a continuous chain of development, with only a micro-mutation between each link. But each link would contain an original invention, the work of an individual.

The chain metaphor is very appropriate, because in making a chain each link has to be separately forged, and it is the same in the making of a style in art. But in art each new link is in some degree different from the last, and though it is joined to the one before it, and will be joined to the one that comes after it, in itself it is unique. That uniqueness is an original invention corresponding to some capacity in the artist, a capacity that is partly a power of observation, partly a power of synthesis.

It seems that we have arrived at this conclusion: originality exists; it can be defined as a capacity to invent *formal* variations in the technique of communication, and a genius might further be defined as an artist who has the capacity to give attractive properties (we call them beauty or magic) to the forms he invents.[17]

Such a generalization is hardly adequate to explain the specific achievements of art. Does it, for example, adequately differentiate originality in the arts from originality in science or technology? Edison was a great and beneficent inventor, but only a materialist would put him on the same level as Cézanne or Picasso. Must we, after all, introduce the element of values?

We shall get into trouble if we do. What values, for example, belong to the art of Cézanne that are not strictly formal? He was not, in any but the most conventional sense, a humanist, or a Christian. He had no message for mankind. An *idea* hardly ever entered his head (except those he got from the newspapers) and he was not even sentimental. He had one criterion of value and one only – his sensibility.

I would suggest that this is true of all great artists, and that even when they have massive intelligences, as Michelangelo had, or Goethe, that is altogether irrelevant. Such great men are artists in spite of their intelligence, not because of it. But there is, of course, no intelligence without sensibility; and when a man is intelligent in the realm of ideas, he is usually sensitive to the values of words, and becomes an artist in words – a poet. Further, although sensibility can exist without intelligence, it may be accompanied by something which is often confused with intelligence – instinctive wisdom.

These generalizations are perhaps best tested in the art of music. I have always been opposed to the idea that music is a special art, with its own aesthetics. Basically all arts have the same aesthetic laws: they differ in the nature of their materials, and in the kind of sensibility required for the formal exploitation of the material.

I am not a musician myself, so I rely on what great musicians have said about their art, and I never find that it contradicts what great painters have said about painting or great poets about poetry. It is only necessary that one should sometimes collate the terminology. If I read a book like Stravinsky's *Poetics of Music*,[18] or Hermann Scherchen's *The Nature of Music*,[19] I at once find rich confirmation of the ideas I have formulated for the plastic arts and poetry. For example, and with reference to our immediate problem, here is Stravinsky:

'Invention presupposes imagination, but should not be confused with it. For the act of invention implies the necessity of a lucky find and of achieving full realization of this find. What we imagine does not necessarily take on a concrete form and may remain in a state of virtuality, whereas invention is not conceivable apart from its actual working out.'

In other words, in music too, invention is a mutation of form in the material, and is not expressive of any ideas or aspirations. And again there is the implication that the invention is not sought, but almost accidentally *found*.

Scherchen confirms this again and again, both in his particular analyses of compositions and in his general statements. He shows, for example, how the structure and episodes of a work like Ravel's *Introduction and Allegro* for solo harp, flute, clarinet and string quartet (1907) are determined by the harp's peculiar technical potentialities. These influence Ravel's melodic idiom, choice of harmonies, and instrumental treatment. 'The medium which inspired him provided an incentive to create new modes of expression, and led Ravel's imagination to find an ethereal shimmering texture never before realized in music. . . . All this is derived – with exquisite imaginative mastery – from the harp's natural sound.'[20]

I introduce music, not so much to confirm what I have already demonstrated from other arts, as to point to the qualities that distinguish all the arts from other mental activities – their super-rational powers of cognition. Of Bach's last composition, the chorale prelude on 'Vor deinem Thron tret'ich hiermit', Scherchen says: 'In listening to this music, one is aware of stimuli far beyond human realization. Bach's last composition demonstrates abilities whose superhuman nature renders them only accessible to genius.' (p. 108.) The same is true, *a fortiori*, of Beethoven's symphonies.

Music is the most originative of the arts because it is a making perceptible of forms that do not exist in nature. Its point of departure may be – perhaps should be – purely imaginative, but the imaginative ideal has to be realized, made concrete, as an audible structure of tones – the reality is something that does not exist physically, the pitch of tones and the intervals between them. The emotive effect, as Scherchen says, is 'to transport the listener beyond the limits of human existence'. He says of art generally that man creates a 'prototype reflecting an order higher than the unreasoning existence of nature'.[21] The importance of music, for our present discussion, is that of all the arts it most clearly shows how an art that is based on sensational elements, acoustical vibrations, can have a meaning that is not in the nature of the medium, but revealed through the medium. A melody exists not in the sounds themselves, but in the pitch and interval which the composer gives to and inserts between the sounds.[22]

The test of greatness in a work of art is, as Scherchen says, that it *transports* us: lifts us out of our temporal existence and holds us suspended in timeless attention. But it has that power, not in virtue of any idea conveyed to the mind in conceptual terms, but by the direct impact on our senses of a highly and subtly organized *material*. A work of art is an organization of sensation rather than a mode of representation. The understanding of art begins and ends with that realization. By this act of transport, this reaching after an order higher than the unreasoning existence of nature, man does not deny life. Art is not an escapist activity. On the contrary, it is the means by which we achieve what Wordsworth called 'the widening the sphere of human sensibility'. This phrase comes from the *Essay Supplementary to the Preface* of 1815, and the whole passage is very relevant to our enquiry:

'If every great poet with whose writings men are familiar in the highest exercise of his genius, before he can be thoroughly enjoyed, has to call forth and communicate *power*, this service, in a still greater degree, falls upon an original writer at his first appearance in the world. – Of genius the only proof is, the act of doing well what is worthy to be done, and what was never done before: Of genius, in the fine arts, the only infallible sign is the widening the sphere of human sensibility, for the delight, honour, and benefit of human nature. Genius is the introduction of a new element into the intellectual universe: or, if that be not allowed, it is the application of powers to objects on which they had not before been exercised, or the employment of them in such a manner as to produce effects hitherto unknown. What is all this but an advance, or a conquest, made by the soul of the poet?'

A conquest for 'the delight, honour and benefit of human nature': these words were well chosen by Wordsworth. Reality, our very poise and equanimity in the universal order, is something we achieve through the organs of perception and sensation. It is not an inevitable possession, as we see when that poise and equanimity are lost, and the mind becomes deranged or unbalanced. A sense of reality is a conquest, an advance from the chaos and confusion of an unintelligible world: a construction. The first order introduced into man's conception of the world was an aesthetic order – the order of ritual and myth. Later the intellect gradually made a selection of the totality – the part it can describe and measure – and gave it a more or less coherent unity, and called it science. The map is constantly enlarged: new details are filled in; but vast territories of space and time must still be marked 'terra incognita'. The sensibility plays like lightning over these dark abysses, and in the flashes gets a brief glimpse of the lineaments of this Unknown: the brief glimpse that is the artist's intuition, and which he then strives to communicate to us by the symbols he invents. That is the moment of originality – the moment in which we are made to realize the ethereal shimmering texture of music, the 'shapes that haunt thought's wildernesses' in poetry, the 'beauty wrought out from within upon the flesh' of a painting. Poetry, painting, music – all these are arts or skills for raising the senses to that condition of insight, in which the world is not transfigured, but in which for the first time some aspect of it is revealed, is given a form, and thereby, for human eyes, newly created, newly communicated.

3. George Stubbs. White Horse frightened by a Lion. 1770

4. *John Constable. Stonehenge. c.1836. (detail)*

II

Beauty and Ugliness

I know nothing sublime which is not some modification of power.
BURKE

I

'Esthetics bores me, doesn't interest me at all', declares one of the
most significant of modern painters. 'The slightest intervention
of esthetics obstructs for me the efficiency of functioning and
spoils the sauce. That is why I try to reject from my works all
that could have the smell of esthetics. People with a short-sighted
view have concluded from this that I enjoy painting ugly objects.
Not at all! I don't worry about their being ugly or beautiful;
furthermore these terms are meaningless for me; I even have the
conviction that they are meaningless for everybody; I don't
believe that these notions of ugliness or beauty have the slightest
foundation: they are illusion.'[1]

Such is the annihilating challenge which M. Jean Dubuffet
hurls at our traditional concepts of beauty and ugliness. In this
paper I propose to ask whether these concepts are indeed meaningless, or whether we can give them new meanings in conformity
with the work of an artist like Dubuffet, who in this respect is
representative of contemporary art in general.

Eranos Jahrbuch, XXX, 1961. Zurich (Rhein Verlag), 1962.

One must begin with the semantic problem, however boring it may be to impatient artists like Dubuffet. The whole discussion has been bedevilled by the inconsistent meanings of the words used in various languages to denote the concept of ugliness. I shall not make a pedantic survey of a confused situation, but if we confine ourselves only to the main division between the Nordic languages and the Mediterranean languages, we find a difference of connotation which makes any direct transfer of the terminology inexact and misleading. The words in the Romance languages derive from the Teutonic root *laipo-* (cf. French *laideur*, Italian *laido*) or the Latin *brutus* (cf. French *brut*, Italian *brutto*) and the original meaning of these words is dull, stupid, senseless – in general the characteristics of animals as compared with rational human beings. Incidentally, the kind of painting practised by Dubuffet is often called in French 'l'art brut'. The Nordic words for ugliness have a very different derivation and connotation: the German *hässlich* is the same root as *hassen*, to hate; whereas the English *ugly* comes from the Middle English *uggen*, or Old Norse *ugga*, fear, or *uggligr*, causing fear, dreadful, terrible.

In Aristotle's *Poetics* and onward through Longinus and Augustine down to the medieval scholastics, the philosophers of the Italian Renaissance and those of the Enlightenment, beauty is conceived as an excellence in the proportion of things: what is not beautiful is what is without perfection of form, or deformed, for which we have the Latin word *turpis*. If we had wanted a word of Latin derivation to describe the contrary of beauty, it should have been 'turpitude'. 'Loathliness' is a possible alternative, and is of the same derivation as the French *laideur* and the Italian *laidezza*. In Scotland and the North of England we have the cognate word 'laidly' – the Laily Worm of the ballad:

> I was bat seven year alld
>   Fan my mider she did dee,
> My father marred the ae warst woman
>   The wardle did ever see.

> For she has made me the laily worm
> That lays att the fitt of the tree,
> An o my sister Messry
> The machrel of the sea.

The father in the ballad discovers his wife's deception and the laily worm is transformed by three strokes of a silver wand into 'the bravest knight Your eyes did ever see', and on the blowing of a small horn the machrel turns into his sister Messry once more. The precise meaning of the word 'laily' or 'laidly' is given when the fish exclaim:

> Ye shaped me ance an unshemly shape
> An ye's never mare shape me.

So we get the same meaning for 'laidly' in English as *laid* has in French: it is a question of form, of deformity, of unshapeliness. This was the original Greek conception of ugliness – the quality of grotesqueness, something misshapen, defective, but not necessarily unaesthetic.[2] Informality is still another concept, which I shall deal with in a later essay (see page 89).

Ugliness in English has always meant something much more positive than that – some quality that causes fear, dread, terror, pain. So when an English philosopher of the Enlightenment such as Edmund Burke, in his *Enquiry into the Origin of our Ideas of the Sublime and Beautiful*, comes to deal with the nature of *Ugliness*, he is compelled to make a distinction which illustrates the confusion inherent in the use of the word as the opposite of beauty:

'But though ugliness be the opposite to beauty, it is not the opposite to proportion and fitness. For it is possible that a thing may be very ugly with any proportions, and with a perfect fitness to any uses. Ugliness I imagine likewise to be consistent enough with an idea of the sublime. But I would by no means insinuate that ugliness of itself is a sublime idea, unless united with such qualities as excite a strong terror.'[3]

Burke's *Enquiry* is a fascinating document in the history of ideas, the arena in which the Greek and the Teutonic concepts of ugliness meet and are reconciled in the idea of the sublime. 'Sublime' itself is the reconciling word, and is an ambiguous rendering of Longinus's Greek word *hypsos*, which means no more than height or elevation. John Hall, the first English translator of Longinus's treatise (1652), gave it the title *On the Height of Eloquence*. 'The Sublime', as Allen Tate in his illuminating essay on Longinus has said, 'carries with it the accretions of Boileau and the English eighteenth century, and the different meanings contributed later by Burke and Kant, which are far removed from anything that I have been able to find in this third – (or is it first) – century treatise'. It is true that Longinus, in his desire to indicate the effect of a heightened style, uses dramatic expressions – the sublime, he suggests, pierces everything 'like a flash of lightning'; and there is his insistence, so welcome to the romantic critic, that some elements of style 'depend upon nature alone' – or as Allen Tate interprets Longinus at this point, 'stylistic autonomy is a delusion, because style comes into existence only as it discovers the subject; and conversely the subject exists only after it is formed by the style'. This, according to Professor Tate, is Longinus's primary insight, and it is one of which Burke made full use.[4]

But Burke, as I must now insist, invests the concept of the sublime with qualities that were far from the mind of Longinus. It would not have occurred to Longinus to make a distinction between the beautiful and the sublime – the whole point of his treatise is to insist that whether by instinct or design, what is excellent in art (and therefore uncommon) is a heightening, an elevation, an intensification of the commonplace. There is ecstasy, but no strangeness, no terror – indeed, '. . . the sublime is often found where there is no emotion'. Far different is Burke's theory, which I will quote in his own summary:

'On closing this general view of beauty, it naturally occurs, that we should compare it with the sublime; and in this comparison there appears a remarkable contrast. For sublime objects are vast in their dimensions, beautiful ones comparatively small; beauty should be smooth, and polished; the great rugged and negligent; beauty should shun the right line, yet deviate from it

6. Rembrandt. The Flayed Ox. 1655

7. Grünewal
Crucifixion. c.151
(deta

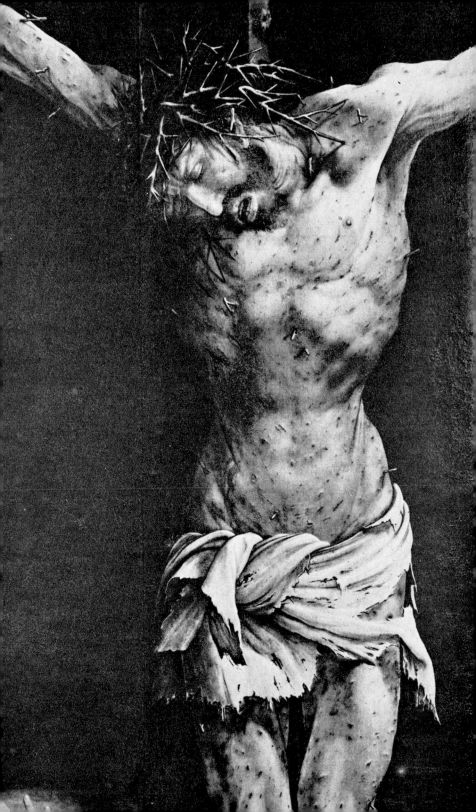

insensibly; the great in many cases loves the right line, and when it deviates, it often makes a strong deviation; beauty should not be obscure, the great ought to be dark and gloomy; beauty should be light and delicate; the great ought to be solid, and even massive. They are indeed ideas of a very different nature, one being founded on pain, the other on pleasure; and however they may vary afterwards from the direct nature of their causes, yet these causes keep up an eternal distinction between them, a distinction never to be forgotten by any whose business it is to affect the passions.'[5]

Vast, rugged, deviating, dark, gloomy and massive – how did Burke visualize such objects of terror and how did he explain their aesthetic effects? Burke, as indeed all philosophers of art before our time, took it for granted that the main principle of art was *mimesis* – that art made its effect by the depiction of objects or events. The examples he gives of the sublime are therefore drawn from nature rather than from literature or the plastic arts: serpents and poisonous animals are capable of raising ideas of the sublime; so is the ocean, darkness and obscurity, and here Burke gives an example from Milton, his description of the King of terrors in *Paradise Lost*:

> The other shape,
> If shape it might be call'd that shape had none
> Distinguishable in member, joynt, or limb,
> Or substance might be call'd that shadow seem'd,
> For each seem'd either; black it stood as Night,
> Fierce as ten Furies, terrible as Hell,
> And shook a dreadful Dart; what seem'd his head
> The likeness of Kingly Crown had on.

'In this description', says Burke, 'all is dark, uncertain, confused, terrible and sublime to the last degree.'

Since terror is increased by obscurity, it is better conveyed by poetry than by painting, for in painting the images tend to be too precise. Milton is quoted again – the famous portrait of Satan from Book I of *Paradise Lost*; and Burke points out that all the

images in this poetical picture – a tower, an archangel, the sun
rising through mists, or in an eclipse, the ruin of monarchs and
the revolution of kingdoms – affect us because they are crowded
and confused. But painting, Burke then admits with an air of
regret, is dependent on the images it presents, and for the most part
these are necessarily precise. He would not have felt the same
about the images of Picasso or Dubuffet.

As a supreme example of sublimity Burke gives a passage in the
Book of Job, where the sublimity 'is principally due to the terrible
uncertainty of the thing described':

> In thoughts from the vision of the night, when deep sleep
> falleth on men, Fear came upon me, and trembling, which
> made all my bones to shake. Then a spirit passed before my
> face; the hair of my flesh stood up: It stood still, *but I could
> not discern the form thereof*; an image was before mine eyes,
> there was silence, and I heard a voice saying, – Shall mortal
> man be more just than God?

And he asks, quite aptly, what painting could possibly rival this
vision wrapt up in the shades of its own incomprehensible darkness. Even those designs of the temptations of St Anthony, 'which
I have chanced to meet', he adds, 'were rather a sort of odd wild
grotesques, than anything capable of producing a serious passion'
(*Plate 8*).

Burke quotes other examples of sublimity from the *Book of Job* –
the horse whose neck is clothed in thunder (*Plate 3*), the wild ass
whose house is the wilderness, the unicorn and the leviathan –
wherever we look upon power, there we find that terror and
sublimity are concomitant. But this is not all – all privations are
terrible, Vacuity, Darkness, Solitude and Silence. Greatness of
dimension, infinity, succession and uniformity which Burke called
'the artificial infinite' (he gives the aisles in many of our old cathedrals as an example, *Plate 45*), sheer magnitude and difficulty (here
Stonehenge – *Plate 4* – is given as an example, where 'the rudeness
of the work increases this cause of *grandeur*, as it excludes the idea
of art, and contrivance'), magnificence (Shakespeare's description

of the King's army in *Henry IV*, Part I), light, or rather excessive brightness (Milton's 'Dark with excessive bright'), certain colours (not soft or cheerful, but sad and fuscous colours, as black, or brown, or deep purple), the noise of vast cataracts, raging storms, thunder or artillery, the shouting of multitudes; a sudden beginning or sudden cessation of sound; and, almost opposite to this, low, tremulous, intermitting sounds; the cries of animals in pain or danger; cups of bitterness, poisonous exhalations – little more need be added to the catalogue, for in conclusion Burke suggests that 'the idea of bodily pain, in all the modes and degrees of labour, pain, anguish, torment, is productive of the sublime; and nothing else in this sense can produce it'. But he adds this acute psychological observation: that the sublime is an idea belonging to self-preservation. The passions which belong to self-preservation are painful when their causes immediately affect us; are delightful (though not pleasurable – Burke distinguishes sharply between delight and pleasure) when we have an idea of pain or danger without being actually involved in the circumstances. That is to say: vicarious ideas of pain, sickness and death fill the mind with strong emotions of horror: they intensify our awareness of life; whereas normal life and health, by simple enjoyment, make no such impression.

We begin to see how the idea of ugliness can be reconciled, not with the pleasure of beauty, but with the delights of sublimity. Ugliness is the physical aspect of certain objects of terror, objects which inspire fear or terror if they are real, but delight if they are counterfeit.

Why should we delight in representations of pain, sickness or death, which fill the mind with horror? The conventional explanation, that the mind is thrilled by an experience which it *knows* to be unreal, is not very convincing. If the mind is constantly aware of the unreality of the enactment, it will remain in a state of ambiguity, and though ambiguity is now a fully recognized aesthetic factor,[6] it is not confined to representations of pain, sickness or death: it can be present in any process of artistic creation and communication. The explanation becomes a little more convincing when it is said that the mind *discovers* the representation that has momentarily inspired fear to be unreal. It is then assumed that the spectator is at first misled into assuming that the enactment of a terrible tragedy is a real event in which he is participating, and is then delighted to discover that it was all pretence. We experience a similar feeling of delight when we awake from a terrifying nightmare and slowly realize that it was all a dream, and that our fears are unnecessary.

We are reminded of Aristotle's theory of *catharsis*, and it may be that modern psychology has not advanced much beyond Aristotle. I do not wish to indulge in a further discussion of this stale subject, but it is perhaps worth emphasizing that Aristotle always insists on the necessity, not only of pity, but also of fear as an element in effective tragedy. When he comes to describe what kind of incidents produce an effect of fear, he makes some extremely interesting qualifications. For example, neither pity nor fear is inspired when an enemy kills his enemy, when the antagonists are strangers to one another. But the situation is very different if such incidents occur between near kinsmen, as when a brother kills a brother, or a son his father; and it is better still, more horrible, more terrifying, if the deed is done in ignorance and the kinship of the person killed is then revealed. One should perhaps note that in this connection Aristotle distinguishes between fear and disgust. Disgust is not tragic, not aesthetic, not sublime.

Sublimity, the elevation of the mind, ought to be the principal end of all our studies, as Burke says, but he recognizes that we cannot go far in these studies without asking questions about the mind itself. In a passage which is one of the earliest anticipations of a theory of the unconscious,[7] Burke suggests that 'a consideration of the rationale of our passions seems to me very necessary for all who would affect them upon solid and sure principles. It is not enough to know them in general; to affect them after a delicate manner, or to judge properly of any work designed to affect them, we should know the exact boundaries of their several jurisdictions; we should pursue them through all their

9. *The Venus of Laussel. France, Palaeolithic period*

11. *Georges Rouault.* *Wrestler* (*The Parade*). *1905*

The Venus of Willendorf. *Austria, Palaeolithic period*

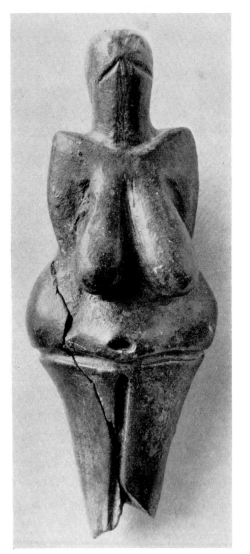

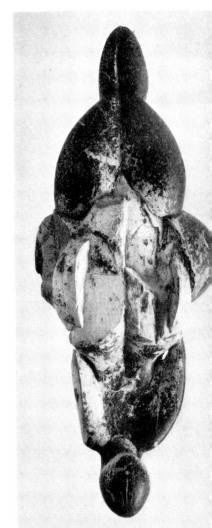

12. *The Venus of Dolní Vestoniče. Czechoslovakia, Gravettian culture*

13. *Ivory Figurine, Lespugue. France, Upper Palaeolithic period*

variety of operations, and pierce into the inmost, and what might appear inaccessible parts of our nature,

Quod latet arcana non enarrabile fibra'

– a line from Persius's *Satires* (V, 29) which might be taken as a still earlier anticipation of the Freudian unconscious.

The full consideration of our subject will inevitably lead us to the unconscious, but before we try to pierce its 'arcana fibra', I would like to describe in more detail the place which ugliness in its fearsome aspects has occupied in the art of the past. I must first deal with the paradox inherent in all this discussion of ugliness. The artist has a certain power of transfiguration. That is to say, he may take an object that is inherently ugly or disgusting – the flayed carcase of an ox, the guillotined head of a criminal, the tortured body of a martyred saint, a crippled idiot or a loathsome reptile, and by painting these subjects with loving care, by giving them aesthetic values of colour and composition, he creates a 'distance' between the reality and our perception which in effect transforms the ugly object into a beautiful work of art. Consider for a moment Grünewald's Isenheim altarpiece (*Plate 7*), the prototype for all such transfigurations. Here is no deformation, no dehumanization: on the contrary, a relentless objectivity or realism. If it is felt that we cannot exclude from our contemplation of such a subject religious emotions which vitally affect our aesthetic responses, then we may substitute Rembrandt's *Flayed Ox* (*Plate 6*) – the aesthetic considerations are identical. In all such works of art we shall find the operation of certain modalities of expression which have the effect of sublimating the object represented. In Aristotle such modalities are called 'poetic diction', and in tragedy we mean that certain subjects or events may be described in verse which could not be described in prose – I have already quoted Burke's examples from *Paradise Lost* and *The Book of Job*. A corresponding process takes place in painting: that is to say, the object, the crucified body of Christ or the flayed ox, is painted with such skill and such delicacy, that we are lost in admiration of the manner, and do not react to the horror of the object itself. The art of the artist by this means creates an aesthetic 'distance' between the crude reality and our organs of perception.

By definition all works of art, whether literary or plastic or musical, must embody an aesthetic principle, and it may be that this factor of 'distance' is always present in a work of art to a greater or lesser degree. But the distinction I want to make is one between works of art which depict the ugly object almost, one might say, with love, accept it in its hideous reality and lift it on to a plane of acceptance; and those works of art which are a deformation of reality, a caricature, grotesque, perverse, in every sense defamatory, and which we accept, if we accept at all, as afflictions, as corrections, as punishments, as a protest. In such cases the deformation is not in the object itself but in the artist's vision of it. In one case the artist accepts the ugliness he finds in nature and redeems it by his art; in the other case the artist by his art creates an ugliness that does not exist in nature, but which nevertheless has positive qualities that fill us with emotions of terror and delight. That ugliness exists in nature and causes us aesthetic displeasure is a remarkable fact but not one which need concern us at the moment. Far more puzzling is the fact that ugliness is deliberately created and seems to satisfy some psychological need. What is the nature of its attractiveness? Why are we fascinated by what is at the same time fearful?

First let me dismiss the assumption, frequently found in traditional aesthetics, that aesthetically speaking such questions are nonsensical. 'All art', asserted one of the most intelligent of English philosophers of art, 'except that of children, savages, ignoramuses and extreme innovators, invariably avoids ugly shapes and seeks for beautiful ones; *but art does this while pursuing all manner of different aims.*'[8] The different aims include 'the awakening, intensifying or maintaining of definite emotional states', but even these 'aids to devotion', as they are called, must presumably avoid ugly shapes. This is simply not true, and to make an exception of 'children, savages, ignoramuses and extreme innovators' is to exclude a vast range of aesthetic experience. Vernon Lee wrote these words in 1912 or 1913, when the art of savages, so called, made a decisive contribution to the foundations of modern art. The tendency that began with Picasso's *Demoiselles d'Avignon* of 1907 was based on a conscious acceptance of ugliness as a positive factor in aesthetic experience. The whole course of the modern movement during the past half-century is almost a reversal of the academic tradition in aesthetics so ably expounded by Vernon Lee (and she bases herself on Fechner, Semper, Lipps, Wundt, and the other founders of this tradition) – indeed we might say that modern art invariably avoids beautiful shapes and seeks for ugly ones. But it is none the less art, and that is the paradox we have to explain.

I must not, however, allow the assumption that it is the art of the past fifty years, and that art alone, which seeks its effects through ugly shapes. Ugliness has always been present in art, from prehistoric times and throughout all subsequent periods. What could be uglier than the Venuses of Laussel and Willendorf (*Plates 9, 10*), representative images from the Palaeolithic period? Only, perhaps, the nudes of Rouault (*Plate 11*) or Beckmann. Mesopotamian art, Egyptian art, Cycladic art, Chinese art, Etruscan art, Gothic art, Renaissance art – in all these epochs we find, not merely depictions of natural ugliness, but wilful deformations of natural objects that are not ugly in themselves. And all this is apart from the art of so-called savage peoples, the tribal art of Africa and Oceania, that contradicts all the canons of beauty which have predominated in our own civilization.

Before seeking the explanation of this paradox, let me give some specific instances. I have already mentioned the palaeolithic Venuses. They are not all ugly – the Venus of Lespugue (*Plate 13*) has had the beauty treatment, is 'stylized', as we say, and conforms to what Vernon Lee calls 'the aesthetic imperative'. The ugly palaeolithic Venuses may be more or less realistic representations of the shapes of pregnant palaeolithic women – similar shapes can be found among the women of primitive tribes in Australia or Africa today. Such carved images were cult objects, and their original purpose was presumably not aesthetic. But we ourselves treat them as rare

examples of the art of prehistoric man: we classify them as works
of art, ugly as they are.

The same is generally true of a vast number of cult objects
characteristic of early civilizations throughout the Near and Far
East – I refer in particular to the sculpture and clay figurines
of Mesopotamia. There is a great variety of style in these
civilizations of the third and second millenia B.C., but one can
distinguish between two types which we might call secular and
sacred. The secular objects, portraits of kings and officials, representations of animals, can easily be assimilated to our ideal of beauty.
But the sacred objects, figures of gods and goddesses, fertility
amulets, objects used in burial rites, etc., are inspired by no such
ideal. Their distortions are designed to strike terror or awe into the
beholder. Describing a group of statues with preternaturally large
eyes found at Tell Asmar and now in the Baghdad Museum,
(*Plate 16*) Professor André Parrot, in his recent book on *Sumer*,
suggests that they may represent a king and queen and high digni-
taries of the city, praying to the gods, in particular to those who
grant fertility and fecundity to the region. 'Their lips are shut, but
the tenseness of the bodies and the keen stare of their eyes are more
eloquent than words. From this petrified group there emanates
something of that awe and apprehension which historians of
religion have described in analysing the sensations primitive man
experiences in the presence of the numinous.'[9]

Awe and apprehension are usually evoked by supernatural
powers and phenomena, but how is it possible that such feelings
can be aroused by human artifacts? I find a difficulty here which
art historians tend to ignore. In discussing one of these same figures
sometimes called the God Abu (*Plate 16*), André Malraux, in his
Introduction to Professor Parrot's book, suggests that such statues
'made the sacred beings present in the spectator's emotion, as
their ideograms made them present in his mind. . . . *The God Abu*
does not suggest a person who might look like him; such a person
is unthinkable. Nor does the company of figures attending him
suggest a *human* assemblage invested with an aura of the sacred,
it is sacred in respect of all that differentiates it from any human

14. *African Sculpture (Bakota).*
Funerary Fetish

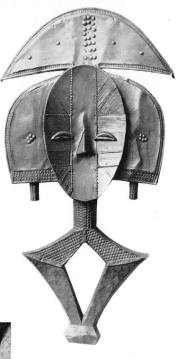

15. *Pablo Picasso.*
Dancer. 1907

16. *The God Abu.*
Mesopotamia.   (detail)

17. *Amorgos.*
Early Cycladic Idol

18. *Ku, the god of War. Hawaiian*

19. *Male Figure. Belgian Congo (Baluba tribe)*

assemblage. For we now know better than to attribute to in-expertness the flagrant disproportion between the tiny hands of the goddess of Tell Asmar and her enormous eyes. During five centuries those strange eyes, with their corneas of bone and eyelids of bitumen, reappear again and again. In making them, the aim of the Sumerian sculptor was not to express himself as an individual; they are means to creation in the fullest sense, since the sculptor was releasing the human figure from man's estate and allying it with the figures of the gods; illuminating a human visage with a gleam of the divine.'[10]

I find it difficult to associate such a transcendental experience with the humble craftsmanship of these objects. It is even difficult to use such language in relation to the work of great geniuses like Michelangelo and Rembrandt. I do not attribute to art a social function less lofty than that which Malraux attributes to it; but when he describes this function as 'the imposition on the visible of a sacred order, as it were a cosmic orchestration, that both orientates men's veneration and frees it from the chaos of appearances', then I must ask: from where does the craftsman get his sacred order, who teaches him the elements of a cosmic orchestration? M. Malraux merely refers us to a communion with the gods. So transcendent is the purpose of art that the artist is unaware of it 'as the saint is unaware of his sainthood'.

I should be in M. Malraux's good company if I were to pass rapidly from Sumer to Egypt, from Egypt to Greece, from Greece to China and Persia, and so through all the many halls in his imaginary museum, dividing the sacred from the secular, beauty from ugliness. But M. Malraux has not used the word 'ugly', and resorts rather to such periphrases as 'the sacred, rendered in a vein of fantasy'. To force the issue I must maintain that if the Adam of Michelangelo is beautiful, if the Hermes of Praxiteles is beautiful, then in the meaning that tradition has given to the word, the god and goddess Abu are ugly, and we are therefore involved in attributing ugliness to the sacred order.

There is, of course, the Manichaean solution to this dilemma. Evil may be as transcendent as holiness, and corresponding to the beauty of holiness we would then naturally assume the existence of the ugliness of evil. That is really the assumption behind the ugliness of Satan in Christian art – the ugliness of all demonology, the iconography of Hell. All religions naturally fall into this antinomial pattern. But before accepting this easy solution of the problem – and it is no solution, but only a convenient statement of it – let us glance in one or two directions where the pattern is not so symmetrical. I find two such disturbing perspectives – one in the realm which for want of a better word we call 'primitive' art; the other in the realm which also for want of a better word we call 'modern' art.

In considering primitive art we must be particularly careful of verbal equivocation. There are rare exceptions, such as the wonderful bronze heads from Ife and Benin, to which we can legitimately apply our concept of beauty, and there may have been historical influences to account for this. But apart from such rare exceptions, this primitive world of art is dominated by terror and fear, and every work of art is (again in our sense of the word) sublimely ugly. There is no antinomy in this world, no antithesis of good and evil, of god and the devil, of Ormuzd and Ahriman. There are various forces immanent and all pervasive.

In African philosophy all being, all essence, in whatever form it is conceived, is conceived not as substance but as force. 'Man is a force, all things are forces, place and time are forces and the "modalities" are forces. Man and woman . . . dog and stone . . . east and yesterday . . . beauty and laughter . . . are forces and as such are related to one another.'[11] The artist is the man who can control these forces and give them formal existence. The work of art is magical because it is an embodiment of the sublime forces that determine all being.

A belief in these forces inspires the whole complex of primitive art. All its formal conventions and modes of representation are conceived in awe and express a desire to tap the sources of a supreme spiritual power.

Let me quote one other authority, but I think the best, for this generalization: Mr William Fagg, of the Department of Ethnography, the British Museum. I do so advisedly, because in the work from which I am to quote he warns us that 'most of those who have written from an aesthetic point of view on African sculpture have succeeded only in interposing an opaque screen of largely irrelevant verbiage between it and the student'.[12] Mr Fagg, in the work in question, who gives a very comprehensive survey of all the varieties of African sculpture, writes of 'the doctrine of force which unites in a single system the three concepts (each having its appropriate art forms) of the worship of gods and spirits, the cult of the ancestors, and the direct harnessing of energy through charms and fetishes'. This is how he describes this informing force:

'It is probable that the most fundamental quality of African sculpture is dynamism; but in trying to apply this concept in art we have passed beyond the field of scientific evidence into one where, for the present, we must rely largely on conjecture and speculation. We know from the plentiful evidence collected by missionaries and anthropologists that the life of many if not most African tribes is pervaded by this concept of dynamism (normally defined as a theory which explains the phenomena of the universe by immanent energy). It has been most explicitly described by Father Placide Tempels in his *Philosophie bantoue* (1947) on the basis of his long researches among the Baluba. . . . According to Tempels, African thought is conditioned by their ontology, that is, their theory of the nature of being: for them being is a process and not a mere state, and the nature of things is thought of in terms of force or energy rather than matter; the forces of the spirit, human, animal, mineral and vegetable worlds are all constantly influencing each other, and by a proper knowledge and use of them a man may influence his own life and that of others. . . . This interpretation of African belief about the nature of things accords well with what we have long known of tribal people in other continents, especially the concept of "soul stuff" in South-East Asia and *mana* in Polynesia. All these peoples seem to share a belief in the desirability of increase in the broadest sense as a principle end of life, together with a corresponding fear of loss of force.'

It will be realized, perhaps, that we have returned to something very near to Burke's concept of the sublime. Burke, of course, had no knowledge of Negro art, but he had a concept of nature, and of the sensationalist basis of our aesthetic reactions, which corresponds very closely to this description of African thought. I would like to recall his definitions:

'The passion caused by the great and sublime in *nature*, when those causes operate most powerfully, is Astonishment; and astonishment is that state of the soul, in which all its motions are suspended, with some degree of horror. In this case the mind is so entirely filled with its object, that it cannot entertain any other, nor by consequence reason on that object which employs it.

'There are many animals who, though far from being large, are yet capable of raising ideas of the sublime, because they are considered as objects of terror. As serpents and poisonous animals of all kinds. And to things of great dimensions, if we annex an adventitious idea of terror, they become without comparison greater. A level plain of a vast extent on land is certainly no mean idea; the prospect of such a plain may be as extensive as a prospect of the ocean; but can it ever fill the mind with anything so great as the ocean itself? This is owing to several causes, but it is owing to none more than this, that the ocean is an object of no small terror.' (*Plate 20.*)

Burke speaks of certain animals in whom the idea of a super-natural force is inherent, and who are therefore terrifying but sublime – the bull and the horse can become sublime in this sense, whereas in the gloomy forest, and in the howling wilderness, are animals like the lion, the tiger, the panther and rhinoceros in whom the terrible and sublime always blaze out together.

Burke gives many other examples of the all-pervasiveness of sublime forces in nature, and these forces are always associated with a sense of vastness and infinity, of fear and astonishment.

20. J. M. W. Turner. *Snowstorm: steamboat off a harbour mouth.* *1842*

21. *Henry Moore. Animal Head. 1951*

He even ventures to contemplate the idea of God, and to argue that his all-pervasive force cannot be separated from the idea of infinite power, and therefore of terror. 'Thus when we contemplate the Deity, his attributes and their operation, coming united on the mind, form a sort of sensible image, and as such are capable of affecting the imagination. Now, though in a just idea of the Deity, perhaps none of his attributes are [*sic*] predominant, yet to our imagination, his power is by far the most striking. Some reflection, some comparing is necessary to satisfy us of his wisdom, his justice, and his goodness; to be struck with his power, it is only necessary that we should open our eyes. But whilst we contemplate so vast an object, under the arm, as it were, of almighty power, and invested upon every side with omnipresence, we shrink into the minuteness of our own nature, and are, in a manner, annihilated before him. And though a consideration of his other attributes may relieve in some measure our apprehensions; yet no conviction of the justice with which it is exercised, nor the mercy with which it is tempered, can wholly remove the terror that naturally arises from a force which nothing can withstand . . . when the prophet David contemplated the wonders of wisdom and power, which are displayed in the economy of man, he seems to be struck with a sort of divine horror, and cries out, *fearfully and wonderfully am I made!*.'[13]

It may seem that I am making an improbable connection between this eighteenth-century philosopher's conception of God and the African native's conception of Nature; but I do not think so: the same all-pervasive power is conceived, capable of inspiring fear and astonishment and capable, through embodiment in sensible images, of striking terror in the beholder. 'A sort of divine horror' is present in both conceptions, and I would maintain that the quality in works of art to which Burke gives the name 'sublime' is identical with that to which the anthropologists give the name 'dynamic energy'. African sculpture, and primitive art generally, can by no means be related to our concept of beauty; I see no difficulty in relating it to this distinct concept of the sublime.

Finally, before I attempt to analyse the sources of this power in our psychological nature, in the economy of man, let me briefly refer to the same concepts in modern art.

The relation of modern art to primitive art is an historical fact: the decisive influence of African sculpture on Picasso (*Plates 14, 15*) and Braque, Brancusi and Henry Moore (*Plate 21*), has been acknowledged by the artists themselves. But apart from that specific instance from 1889 onwards, when primitive art was first exhibited in Europe, a general assimilation of the formal qualities of African, Oceanic, American Indian, Mexican and other primitive types of art began to take place, until a point was reached when the whole of the so-called modern movement abandoned the traditional concept of beauty and moved over to this alternative concept which Burke called the sublime. One does not often think of modern art as sublime; but remembering the definitions made by Burke which I have quoted, there can be no doubt that in its general characteristics it closely conforms to his idea of an irrational and violent experience. Again and again modern artists have disowned the concept of the beautiful. 'Art', Picasso once said, 'is not the application of a canon of beauty but what the instinct and the brain can conceive beyond any canon.'[14] 'Beauty', Henry Moore once wrote, 'in the later Greek or Renaissance sense, is not the aim of my sculpture. Between beauty of expression and power of expression there is a difference of function. The first aims at pleasing the senses, the second has a spiritual vitality which for me is more moving and goes deeper than the senses.'[15] In these forthright denials of beauty two of the most representative masters of the modern movement at the same time assert a positive aim that goes beyond sensuous pleasure, to affirm vitality, intensity, and that 'sort of divine horror' which their works, in their extreme limits, relentlessly inspire.

In order to understand this turning away from beauty and pleasure, this frenetic deformation and disfiguration of the fair face of nature, we must turn our attention inwards, to the psyche, where all images are made and unmade, where pleasure and delight, fear and affliction, alternate in endless dialectical rhythm, like those hammers of the Cyclops described by Virgil in the *Aeneid*, a passage which Burke quotes in another context and provides this translation:

'Three rays of twisted showers, three of watery clouds, three of fire, and three of the winged southwind; then mixed they in the work terrific lightnings, and sound, and fear, and anger, with pursuing flames.'[16]

Vulcan, or Hephaestus, is the archetypal artist and his forged thunderbolts are deliverances of fear with which we readily associate the idea of the sublime. Significantly enough for our argument, Vulcan, deformed, lame and dishevelled, is also the archetype of ugliness.

2

> *Greek art has taught us that there are no truly beautiful surfaces without dreadful depths.*　　NIETZSCHE

The story of 'Beauty and the Beast', 'La Belle et la Bête', was written by Madame Leprince de Beaumont, who was born at Rouen in 1711 and died near Annecy in 1780. It immediately became a very popular fairy-tale, was translated into all languages, and the name of the authoress was forgotten. On a modest scale she had given the world what Sophocles and Shakespeare and Goethe gave it – an archetypal myth. Let me recall some of the details of her story.

Once upon a time there lived a very rich merchant who had six children, three boys and three girls. Of the daughters all were beautiful, but, as in *King Lear*, the two elder ones were proud and selfish; whereas the youngest one, who was called Beauty, was modest and refused all offers of marriage because she was devoted to her father.

The merchant suddenly lost all his wealth except a small house in the country, to which they retired. This reversal of fortune was very disagreeable to the two eldest daughters, but Beauty resolved to try and be happy in spite of their poverty. While her father and brothers worked on the land, she did the housework and the cooking, and in the evening she would read, or play the harpsichord, or sing at the spinning-wheel. Her sisters remained idle and discontented.

After living in poverty for a year the merchant heard that one of his ships, which he had believed lost, had returned to port laden with merchandise. The merchant set off for the port, first asking his daughters what they would like him to bring back for them. The two eldest asked for rich dresses and jewels, but Beauty asked only for a rose – 'for none grows here'.

When he arrived at the port the merchant found that all his goods had been distrained by his creditors, so he had to go back home as poor as when he had set out. It was only about thirty miles to his house, but he had to pass through a great wood in which he lost his way. It was snowing heavily and blowing so hard that twice he fell from his horse. Suddenly at the end of a long cutting in the trees, he saw a bright light shining ahead of him; so he led his horse towards it and came to a great castle all lit up. There was no one about, but there was an open stable full of hay and oats upon which his hungry horse fell with avidity. He himself entered the castle and in the great hall found a fire burning and a table laden with food, and laid only for one guest. He dried himself before the fire, and waited some time, but no one appeared. Unable to resist the pangs of hunger any longer, he devoured a chicken, drank several glasses of wine and then went off in search of a bed, which he found and on which he lay down and slept.

When he awoke at ten o'clock next morning he found everything prepared for him, clean clothes and a cup of hot chocolate. Outside the snow had disappeared and the garden was bright with flowers. He went out to look for his horse, and in passing by a bed of roses suddenly remembered Beauty's request. He stooped to pick one, and at that moment there was a terrible roar, and looking up he saw a hideous beast, so horrible that he nearly fainted. 'How ungrateful you are', roared the Beast. 'I saved your life by taking you into my castle, and in return for my hospitality you steal my roses, which I love better than anything in the world. You must therefore die to expiate your crime and I shall give you only a quarter of an hour to make your peace with God.' The poor merchant threw himself upon his knees – 'My lord', he pleaded, 'I did not think I would offend you so gravely by plucking a rose for one of my daughters, who had asked me to bring her one.'

'I am not a lord', replied the monster, 'I am a Beast. I do not like compliments. I prefer people who say what they think, and you do not move me with your flattery. But since you tell me you have some daughters, I will forgive you on condition one of them comes here willingly to die in your stead. Do not argue with me; go immediately, but before you go, swear that in three months you will return if meanwhile one of your daughters does not come to die in your place.'

The merchant gave this promise and then the Beast told him to return to his chamber and fill the chest he would find there with anything that took his fancy and the Beast would have it carried to his house. He went to the room and filled the chest with gold.

The merchant then mounted his horse, which found its own way through the forest paths without difficulty. Within a few hours the good man was at home again being greeted by his excited children. To Beauty he gave the rose, saying: 'Take it; it cost your father very dear.' He then told them the whole story.

The elder sisters turned on Beauty with all kind of insults, but in the end Beauty, on her own insistence, returned to the castle with her father and the same welcome awaited them. When they had finished supper there was a great roar and the Beast appeared and asked Beauty if she had come of her own free will. On replying that it was so, the Beast turned to the father and told him he must return the next morning, leaving his daughter behind. They then went to bed and in the morning the father full of remorse said goodbye to his daughter.

Then begins the Beast's wooing of Beauty in this enchanted

castle. Gradually Beauty was overwhelmed with sympathy for the
poor Beast, because he was so kind to her, and in the end she grew
accustomed to his ugliness. But when he asked her to be his wife,
she could but refuse, much to the distress of the Beast. Finally
she asked if she might return home to see her father, for in a magic
mirror in her room she had seen that he was ill and pining.
Reluctantly the Beast allowed her to go home but told her that
she must return at the end of a week or he would pine away.

Beauty was then transported to her home where she rejoined
her joyful father and her jealous sisters. The sisters were so envious
that they plotted to keep Beauty beyond the permitted week, in
the hope that the Beast would be so angry that he would then
devour her. Beauty was prevailed upon to stay one more week,
but on the tenth night she dreamt that she was back in the castle
garden and that she saw the Beast lying prostrate on the grass.

Full of pity for the Beast, the next morning, thanks to a magic
ring the Beast had given her for the purpose, she found herself
back in the castle and waited for the Beast to appear. But he did
not appear; so she searched everywhere in the castle, and then,
remembering her dream, ran down the garden and found him
lying there unconscious. His heart was still beating and she
revived him by sprinkling water on his forehead. The Beast
opened his eyes and told Beauty that he no longer wanted to live
since she had forgotten her promise. 'Oh my dear Beast, you must
not die', cried Beauty, 'but live and marry me. I thought that it
was only friendship I felt for you, but the grief I felt when I
thought you were dead made me see that I cannot live without
you.'

No sooner had Beauty said these words than the whole castle
lit up, with fireworks and music. The Beast had disappeared and
in his place she saw a Prince more beautiful than Love himself.
A wicked fairy, the Prince explained, had cast a spell on him and
he had to remain in the form of a Beast until a beautiful girl
offered to marry him. A transformation scene follows, complete
with a fairy, who says to Beauty: 'Come and receive the reward
for the choice you have made; you have preferred virtue to beauty

and wit, and you now deserve to find all these qualities in the one you love. You will become a great queen; may your throne not destroy your virtue.' The elder sisters are duly admonished, the marriage takes place in the Prince's Kingdom, and they lived a very long time in perfect happiness because their love was founded on virtue.

This story has certain parallels with other legends and fairy-tales, such as 'Cinderella' and Andersen's 'Ugly Duckling', but for our purpose it is the most perfect constellation of archetypal images. To begin with, we have two sets of triads, one male (the three brothers), one female (the three sisters), which for each sex may be said to represent three of the four functions of consciousness. To acquire wholeness it is necessary to discover and make conscious the fourth function, which is buried in the unconscious (represented in our fairy-tale by the great castle hidden in the woods). But this fourth function is disguised in an ugly shape and, before it can be united with the other functions, must be transformed. The symbol of transformation is 'the flower of peace, the Rose that cannot wither',[17] but the rose cannot be plucked, the love cannot be consummated, until certain conditions have been fulfilled. The essential test is that ugliness itself should be spontaneously loved, and this is brought about by the kindness of the Beast, which is contrasted with the envy of Beauty's two sisters, who do everything they can to thwart the union of Beauty and the Beast.

In the story we also find certain subsidiary objects which have a symbolic value such as the chest which the father was allowed to fill with gold, and which was magically transported to his house, and the magic mirror in which, while a prisoner in the castle (the unconscious), Beauty could see her absent father. It would not serve my immediate purpose to enlarge on the significance of these symbols. What is important for our present discussion is the dramatic symbolization of the four functions of consciousness.

Let me first remind the reader of Jung's classic description of the four functions in *The Structure and Dynamics of the Psyche*:[18]

'Consciousness is primarily an organ of orientation in a world of outer and of inner facts. First and foremost, it establishes the fact that something is there. I call this faculty *sensation*. By this I do not mean the specific activity of any of the senses, but perception in general. Another faculty interprets what is perceived; this I call *thinking*. By means of this function, the object perceived is assimilated and its transformation into a psychic content proceeds much further than in mere sensation. A third faculty establishes the value of the object. This function of evaluation I call *feeling*. The pain-pleasure reaction of feeling marks the highest degree of subjectivation of the object. Feeling brings subject and object into such a close relationship that the subject must choose between acceptance and rejection.'

(At this point let me observe how perfectly our fairy-tale illustrates this point: it is the growth of sympathetic feeling in Beauty's consciousness that enables her to choose between acceptance and rejection of the Beast.)

To continue with Jung's description: 'These three functions could be quite sufficient for orientation if the object in question were isolated in space and time. But, in space, every object is in endless connection with a multiplicity of other objects; and, in time, the object represents merely a transition from a former state to a succeeding one. Most of the spatial relationships and temporal changes are unavoidably unconscious at the moment of orientation, and yet, in order to determine the meaning of an object, space-time relationships are necessary. It is the fourth faculty of consciousness, *intuition*, which makes possible, at least approximately, the determination of space-time relationships. This is a function of perception which includes subliminal factors, that is, the possible relationship to objects not appearing in the field of vision, and the possible changes, past and future, about which the object gives no clue. Intuition is an immediate awareness of relationships that could not be established by the other three functions at the moment of orientation.'

The integration of the personality implies a conscious awareness and balance of all four functions. But it often happens in our psychological experience 'that three of the four functions can become differentiated, i.e. conscious, while the other remains connected with the matrix, the unconscious, and is known as the "inferior" function'. It is (as Jung observes in another context) 'the Achilles heel of even the most heroic consciousness; somewhere the strong man is weak, the clever man foolish, the good man bad, and the reverse is also true'.[19] In our story, the beautiful man is ugly, and that is what our story is about: the transformation of ugliness into beauty, of blindness into perception, so that the four functions of consciousness can achieve perfect unity.

The function inhibited in 'Beauty and the Beast' is feeling, but the story makes it clear that space-time relationships are also involved, as in most fairy-tales. They will be resolved at the moment of orientation, which is the scene of transformation.

Let us now ask why a wicked fairy has cast a spell of ugliness on a Prince 'more beautiful than Love himself'. The wicked fairy represents the drive that has produced a dissociation of consciousness, a complex, as we call it, and has substituted, in the field of perception, this unpleasant object, the ugly Beast. Beauty in her feminine consciousness has encountered a masculine counterpart, a hideous animus. But the father, too, is aware of the Beast's ugliness; indeed, it was the father who first penetrated the castle, the unconscious, and found there the rose of Peace guarded by the terrifying Beast. The daughter becomes a father substitute, a daughter distinguished from her sisters by her lack of envy. This daughter is prepared to die for her father. Incidentally, in the story, it is from her father that she first receives the symbolic rose, which the Beast had allowed him to bring away from the castle.

It is tempting to interpret the Beast as the Shadow, that archetype of the dark aspects of the personality, the negative side of the psyche, but according to Jung's conception of this archetype, it is always of the same sex as the subject: it represents first and foremost the personal unconscious. The contrasexual archetype in a woman is the animus, a male principle. Why, in this fairy-tale, is it rejected: why is it ugly?

To find an explanation of this paradox I think we shall have to
leave the sphere of Jungian psychology and take hints from some
later developments of Freudian psychology; but first let us note
that Jung does admit, parenthetically, that the father is the factor
involved in the projection of the animus for the daughter, just
as the mother is the factor for the son.[20] Jung also points out that
these archetypes are often projected in the form of animals. But
why as an ugly monster?

According to Freud, the early stages of the Oedipus conflict
are dominated by sadism. They fall within a phase of development
which is inaugurated by oral sadism and terminates when the
ascendancy of anal sadism comes to an end.[21] In *Beyond the Pleasure
Principle* Freud relates how he came to modify his earlier hypothesis of a polymorphous sexual instinct and substituted an opposition between two kinds of instinct, one kind being directed
towards an 'object', the other towards the ego. Then, from further
researches into the libido-development of the child in its earliest
phases, it became clear that the ego is the true and original
reservoir of the libido, 'which is extended to the object only from
this. The ego took its place as one of the sexual objects and was
immediately recognized as the choicest among them. Where the
libido remained attached to the ego, it was termed "narcissistic".'[22] The difference between these two kinds of instinct,
which had formerly been regarded as qualitative, now had to be
defined topographically, and a neurosis could then be seen as the
result of a conflict between the ego and the libidinous investment
of an object. The main development of Freudian psycho-analysis
seems to have been an investigation of this hypothesis. Freud's own
final position was based on a sharp distinction between the libido
and the death instinct, which he renamed Eros and Thanatos.
As a further consequence of this hypothesis, Freud suggested
that 'object-love itself displays a second such polarity, that of
love (tenderness) and hate (aggression)'. A sadistic component
in the sexual instinct was recognized, and as a perversion this
can attain independence and dominate the sexual life of a
person.

Freud pointed out that in infancy, at the oral stage of organization of the libido, amorous possession is still one and the same as annihilation of the object, and it is this aspect of psychic development that Melanie Klein took up with such fervour. Her own summary of the matter will lead us straight to the point I wish to make:

'In his book *Beyond the Pleasure Principle*, Freud put forward a theory according to which at the outset of the life of the human organism the instinct of aggression, or the death-instinct, is being opposed and bound by the libido, or life-instinct – the eros. A fusion of the two instincts ensues, and gives rise to sadism. In order to escape being destroyed by its own death-instinct, the organism employs its narcissistic or self-regarding libido to force the former outward, and direct it against its objects. Freud considers this process as fundamental for the person's sadistic relations to his objects. I should say, moreover, that parallel with this deflection of the death-instinct outward against objects, an intra-psychic reaction of defence goes on against that part of the instinct which could not be thus externalized. For the danger of being destroyed by this instinct of aggression sets up, I think, an excessive tension in the ego, which is felt by it as an anxiety, so that it is faced at the very beginning of its development with the task of mobilizing libido against its death-instinct. It can, however, only imperfectly fulfil this task, since, owing to the fusion of the two instincts, it can no longer, as we know, effect a separation between them. A division takes place in the id, or instinctual levels of the psyche, by which one part of the instinctual impulses is directed against the other.

'This apparently earliest measure of defence on the part of the ego constitutes, I think, the foundation-stone of the development of the super-ego, whose excessive violence in this early stage would thus be accounted for by the fact that it is an offshoot of very intense destructive instincts, and contains, along with a certain proportion of libidinal impulses, very large quantities of aggressive ones.

'This view of the matter makes it also less puzzling to understand why the child should form such monstrous and phantastic
images of his parents. For he perceives his anxiety arising from
his aggressive instincts as fear of an external object, both because
he has made that object their outward goal, and because he has
projected them on to it so that they seem to be initiated against
himself from that quarter.'[23]

We have now, I hope, sufficient material for a psycho-analytical
interpretation of our fairy-tale. The Beast is the image of those
sadistic and destructive instincts which accumulate in the child's
ego in the course of its early development, particularly during the
first four years, when, as Melanie Klein says, we come across a
super-ego of the most incredible and phantastic character. 'We
get to look upon the child's fear of being devoured, or cut up,
or torn to pieces, or its terror of being surrounded and pursued
by menacing figures, as a regular component of its mental life;
and we know that the man-eating wolf, the fire-spewing dragon,
and all the evil monsters out of myths and fairy-stories flourish
and exert their unconscious influence in the phantasy of each
individual child, and it feels itself persecuted and threatened by
those evil shapes.'[24] Madame Leprince de Beaumont had the
ability to recover such an image from her childhood memories,
and to exorcise it by a myth of transformation. But the figure of
the Beast is an image of the mother (who, significantly, has no
place in the fairy-tale) projected with all the psychic significance
of the narrator's archetypal animus: the mother who had had the
power to grant or withhold the gratification of her needs, the
externalized symbol of the death instincts, terrifying to Eros until
transformed by the magic of love. The story seems to assume that
at some earlier stage the daughter had been deprived of the
mother's breast and her libido had therefore turned towards the
father.

Aesthetic pleasure has been defined (by Adrian Stokes[25]) as 'the
perception of a reconstructed whole . . . one built upon the
recognition of the object's previous loss or ruin (whether or not

this ruin is also shown) in contrast with manic denial. Art, if only by implication, bears witness to the world of depression or chaos overcome.' *Beauty and the Beast* is a perfect allegory of such reconstruction or restitution. Ugliness (the Beast) we have previously defined as that which is unshapely, but as Burke warned us, it is not the opposite to proportion or fitness: it is consistent with an idea of the sublime, of *terribilità*. John Rickman, who was the first to look at the nature of ugliness from a psycho-analytical point of view, suggested that just as human psychology made greater progress when it gave recognition to the factors of mental pain, anxiety and guilt, so it would 'seem prudent to accord more significance than is commonly done in the literature to these disturbing but powerful forces in our aesthetic inclinations, and to see whether the underlying impulses of destructiveness, which give rise to these painful feelings, do not provide a sub-stratum to Art as they do to everyday life. . . . The artist provides more than a momentary consolation for our miseries; he goes behind the veil which screens the source of our dejection and brings back evidence for the triumph of the creative impulse over the forces of destruction; he can do this not by the denial of pain but by facing it with a determination to master it.'[26] But there is more to it than therapy and reparation, which indeed Rickman indicated in the final words of his paper: 'Our need for beauty springs from the gloom and the pain we experience from our destructive impulses to our good and loved objects; our wish is to find in art evidence of the triumph of life over death; we recognize the power of death when we say a thing is ugly.'

Dr Hanna Segal, developing this theory twelve years later,[27] defined ugliness as that which 'expresses the state of the internal world in depression. It includes tension, hatred and its results – the destruction of good and whole objects and their change into persecutory fragments.' Depression is a technical term in Kleinian analysis, derived from the loss of the loved object, the breast: a very complex group of anxieties. Dr Segal is much more realistic, and more faithful to the aesthetic experience, because she recognizes that Rickman's definition does not allow for the continued presence of ugliness in the work of art: it assumes that ugliness is the contrary to beauty and must be transformed before there can be a satisfying aesthetic experience. But altogether apart from the ugly works of art I have mentioned, the ugly is always nakedly present in tragedy, even in comedy; indeed, in Dr Segal's words, 'the idea that ugliness is an essential component of a complete experience seems to be true of the tragic, the comic, the realistic, in fact of all the commonly accepted categories of the aesthetic except one' – 'classical' beauty. And even in this case 'all our analytical experience as well as the knowledge derived from other forms of art suggest that the deep experience (embodied in the classical work of art) must have been what we call, clinically, a depression, and that the stimulus to create such a perfect whole must have lain in the drive to overcome an unusually strong depression'.

All this is in agreement with an aesthetics of the work of art which stems from Lipps and Riegl and is most succinctly represented by Worringer's theory of abstraction and empathy. As long ago as 1908, that is to say, long before the diffusion of the psycho-analytical theories we have discussed, Worringer wrote of 'the polar antithesis between two forms of aesthetic enjoyment' – of, on the one hand, 'the ego as the clouding of the greatness of a work of art, as a curtailment of its capacity for bestowing happiness', and, on the other hand, 'the most intimate union between ego and work of art, which receives all its life from the ego alone'. Further: 'This dualism of aesthetic experience . . . is . . . not a final one. These two poles are only gradations of a common need, which is revealed to us as the deepest and ultimate essence of all aesthetic experience – the need for self-alienation.' Popular usage, as Worringer points out, speaks with striking accuracy of 'losing oneself' in the contemplation of a work of art. In this sense we can attribute all aesthetic enjoyment to the impulse of self-alienation. The need for empathy and the need for abstraction are the two poles of human aesthetic experience, one representing the only possibility of repose, not only from the confusion and obscurity of the external world, but also from the confusion and obscurity of the internal world in depression; the other representing immersion in the immediate and the organic, the condition being that the work of art reflects natural organic tendencies in man and permits him, in Worringer's words, 'in aesthetic perception, to flow uninhibitedly with his inner feeling of vitality, with his inner need for activity, into the felicitious current of this formal happening. So that, borne along by this inexpressible, inapprehensible movement, he experiences that absence of desire which makes its appearance the moment man – delivered from the differentiation of the individual consciousness – is able to enjoy the unclouded happiness of his purely organic beings.'[28]

This dualism corresponds to the facts of the history of art, and though the antitheses, in principle, are mutually exclusive (as we might demonstrate in the extremes of contemporary art, expressionism and constructivism), nevertheless in actual fact, as Worringer again points out, 'the history of art represents an unceasing disputation between the two tendencies'.[29] Personally I have always clung to the supposition, as Ruskin did, that there is a possibility of reconciliation, of synthesis: that all the many antitheses or oppositions we use to describe our psychological and aesthetic experiences – abstraction and empathy, style and naturalism, form and feeling, beautiful and ugly – all these in certain rare works of art find a perfect balance. Ruskin thought he had found that balance in what he called a piece of 'mathematic sculpture', the tomb of Ilaria del Caretto in Lucca Cathedral carved in the year 1406 by Jacopo della Quercia (*Plate 23*); of which he wrote[30] that it is the only piece of monumental work known to him in the world 'which unites in perfect and errorless balance the softest mysteries of emotion with the implacable severities of science'. The mysteries of emotion revealed by psycho-analysis can hardly be described as 'soft'; nor does science in aesthetic form remain implacably severe; but that integration of the personality which is the aim of psycho-analysis, and that 'reserve and restraint of power' represented in a work of art such

as the tomb of Ilaria, is perfectly symbolised in the marriage of
Beauty and the Beast.

'Beauty', said the fairy in our story, 'come and receive the
reward for the choice you have made; you have preferred virtue
to beauty and wit, and now you deserve to find all these qualities
in the one you love. You will become a great queen; may your
throne not destroy your virtue.'

There is an epilogue to the story. Integral to the fairy-tale are
the two sisters of Beauty, whose hearts, as we have already noted,
were full of envy. I cannot now enlarge on the significance of
envy in psycho-analysis, but it is fundamental. It is the factor that
destroys human happiness and it has its roots in the Oedipal
situation. When in the story the father returned from the castle
for the first time, he brought with him the rose that Beauty had
asked for, and when he gave it to her, he said: 'Here you are,
Beauty, take this rose. It has cost your father very dear.' The two
sisters then turned on Beauty and heaped all the blame upon her.
'See', they cried, 'what this miserable little creature's pride has
brought us to! Why couldn't she ask for sensible things as we
did! But oh no, Miss Beauty must always be different. And now
she has been the means of condemning our father to death, she
doesn't even weep.'

The rose is a symbol of what all the sisters desire, but which
only Beauty has succeeded in obtaining. This is the basis of the
intense envy of the elder sisters. When at the end of the story the
fairy turns to them, she says: 'I know your little hearts and all the
the malice they contain. You will become two statues, yet keep
your reason within the stone that shall embalm you. You will
stand forever at the gate of your sister's castle and I impose no
other punishment on you than this: that you must watch and witness her happiness. You can break the spell the moment you
recognize your own faults, but I'm very much afraid you will
always remain as statues. For though one may correct pride, bad
temper, greediness and sloth, only a miracle can take envy from
the heart.'

And that is the conclusion of the analysts about feminine envy

22. *La Belle et la Bête. From the film directed by Jean Cocteau. 1946*

23. *Jacopo della Quercia. Tomb of Ilaria del Caretto. c.1406*

in general. Only a miracle, a strong incentive combined with a capacity for self-sacrifice such as Beauty manifested, gives a woman, wrote Melanie Klein,[31] in individual instances, the capacity for such a very exceptional achievement as the overcoming of what is known as the castration complex, the deep source of envy and sadism. This may explain, not only the prevalence of envy in the feminine heart, but also the comparative rarity of works of art created by women.

III

The Origins of Form in the Plastic Arts

I

Form in art is the shape imparted to an artifact by human intention and action. In English 'form' seems to have an aesthetic connotation not carried by the word 'shape', but *shape*, which is cognate with the Old English *sceapan* and the German *schaffen*, better conveys the creative implications of this human activity. Form is also given to natural objects, either by the process of growth, or by crystallization or other physical changes, and there is a whole science of form in nature which we call morphology, after the Greek word for form. But there is no distinct science dealing with form in human artifacts, though these have distinctive laws or habits of perfection.

Form, as I shall discuss it, must be distinguished from composition. I shall not be concerned with the relation of parts to a whole, or to the laws of harmony and proportion that govern their interrelations. Of course, every form can be measured, and one can discuss the harmonic significance of these measurements, or their lack of harmony. But the interesting problem, and one to which practically no attention has ever been directed, is the origins of the very concept of form in art. Why, out of the shapeless chaos of sticks and stones, or out of the handy and useful objects which were the first tools of primitive man, did form

Eranos Jahrbuch, XXIX, 1960. Zurich (Rhein Verlag), 1961.

progressively emerge until it surpassed the utilitarian purpose of the shaped object and became a form for the sake of form, that is to say, a work of art?

I am perhaps already begging the question, but I will clarify it by some precise illustrations from the artifacts of prehistoric man. Man is first differentiated in the process of evolution by an ability to make tools. It has been proved by Professor Wolfgang Köhler in his famous experiments with chimpanzees that apes are capable of improvising tools, but this only happens when the animal is incited by the prospect of a *visible* reward. The ape lacks two components of thought upon which man's tool-making depends: the power of combining mental images – in short, imagination – and the power of speech and the conceptual process that results from speech. This is perhaps not immediately obvious, but Dr Kenneth Oakley of the British Museum of Natural History has recently reduced the considerable research on this subject to the following cautious statement:

'One may sum up by saying that apes of the present day are capable of perceiving the solution of a visible problem, and occasionally of improvising a tool to meet a given situation; but to conceive the idea of shaping a stone or a stick for use in an imagined future eventuality is beyond the mental capacity of any known apes. Possession of a great capacity for this conceptual thinking, in contrast to the mainly perceptual thinking of apes and other primates, is generally regarded by comparative psychologists as distinctive of man. Systematic making of tools implies a marked capacity for conceptual thought.'[1]

The recent experiments in training chimpanzees to paint do not contradict such a conclusion. Congo, the chimpanzee in the London Zoo trained by Dr Desmond Morris,[2] did produce amazingly effective paintings, but not only were the colours pre-selected by the scientists in charge of the experiments, but they were presented to the chimpanzee one by one, and the paper on which he painted was usually withdrawn to allow each colour to dry separately, and so safeguard against any accidental tendency to mix the colours. The design is due to a combination of random muscular actions and automatic perceptual processes – a 'good *Gestalt*' may result, as indeed it does from various automatic painting machines that have been invented during recent years. But again, there is no capability of combining images, no shaping power of the imagination.

If we turn now to the first objects deliberately shaped by man, which are tools of various kinds, we find a chronological sequence which begins with convenient pieces of sharp stone, sharks' teeth or shells, anything with a cutting edge, and gradually (over many thousands of years) leads to objects deliberately shaped for this purpose.[3] The earliest tools are known as eoliths (dawn-stones) and are indistinguishable from the accidents of nature. Such stones are still used by Australian tribes. The problem of distinguishing these eoliths from deliberately shaped tools need not concern us: we may merely note that there gradually appear various types of stone implements that are unmistakably shaped by human agency (*Plates 24-27*). Usually of flint, they have been produced by flaking the natural stone. The flint is sharply tapped at a point on the surface with the result that a flake of a certain size is chipped off, and by progressive blows at the right points, the required shape is produced – the shape required by the function of the tool. The process could give two possible end-results: the flake that was removed from the flint, and the core of flint from which flakes had been removed. Either might be utilized as a tool, the flake as a scraper, the core as a hand-axe.

Once the process had been invented, then the way was open for a continuous refinement of skill and of the tools produced by the skill, this process of refinement going hand-in-hand with the choice of more effective materials and the invention of new methods of working. It should be realized, however, that an immense period of time stretches between the earliest appearance of the pear-shaped hand-axe, the distinctive tool of the Lower Palaeolithic period in Europe (*c.* 550,000 to 250,000 years ago) and the invention of the refined tools of the Neolithic period (*c.* 3000 to 1500 B.C.; *Plates 28, 31, 32*). Something like half a

24. *Flint hand-axe from the Thames Valley.   Lower Palaeolithic period*

25. *Polished flint hand-axe from Bornholm.   Late Neolithic period*

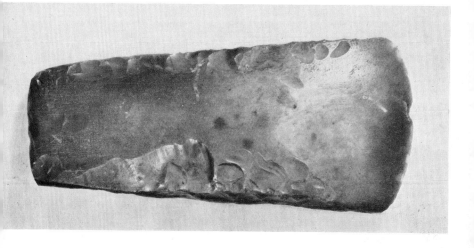

26. *Ripple-flaked flint knife from Egypt. c.4000 BC*

27. *Ripple-flaked flint knife from Egypt. Pre-dynastic period*

28. *Neolithic flint dagger from Denmark. c.1500–1200 BC*

30a. *Jade ritual halberd blade.*
Chinese, Shang-Ying period

30b. *Ceremonial halberd. Chinese,*
late Shang or Early Chou Dynasty

29. *Jade ritual halberd blade.*
Chinese, before 1000 BC

31. *Polished axe-head from Ireland. Neolithic period*

32. *Ritual axe-head. Chinese, Neolithic period*

million years of experience in stone precedes the swift elaboration of iron and bronze. But once iron had replaced stone, and bronze had replaced (or been added to) iron, man had at his command the technical means for the establishment of an enduring civilization.

In order to get a clearer idea of the formal or morphological evolution of these artifacts, it would be best to divide them into three types: (1) piercing and cutting implements, where sharpness is the guiding motive; (2) hammering or bludgeoning implements, where concentrated mass and power is the purpose; and (3) hollow vessels to be used as containers of a food. We shall then find that although the purposes are different, the morphological evolution proceeds along parallel lines.

There can be no possible doubt that for long periods of time the drive behind such evolution was for efficiency. There can equally be no doubt that the search for efficiency led imperceptibly to forms which were not only efficient, but also, for our modern sensibility, beautiful. In any long sequence of axe-heads or spear-heads or arrow-heads there is a progressive refinement of shape due to increasing skill in flaking, then in abrading and polishing, until finally we have artifacts of such elegance that it is not reasonable to suppose they could have been intended as practical tools. Archaeologists distinguish between several Palaeolithic cultures on the basis of the prevailing tools – for example, pebble-tool and hand-axe cultures, chopper-tool cultures, flake-tool and blade-tool cultures, but I do not think these need concern us, because whatever the tool, and whatever the material, the process of refinement was the same. We must not exclude, of course, the possibility of periods of degeneration.

What I would like to establish, for all these early human arti-facts, is an evolutionary sequence that passes through three stages: (1) conception of the object as a tool; (2) making and refinement of the tool to a point of maximum efficiency; (3) refinement of the tool beyond the point of maximum efficiency towards a conception of form-in-itself. The evolution from the first to the second stage is not in doubt; it is the normal cultural sequence as established by palaeontologists and archaeologists. But in what manner, and for what reason, did man quite early in his cultural development, and long before historical times, pass from functional form to form-in-itself, that is to say, to aesthetic form?

There are two possible hypotheses that might lead us towards an explanation of the origins of aesthetic form. The first might be called *naturalistic* or *mimetic*, the second perhaps *idealistic*. According to the first hypothesis, all formal deviations from efficiency would be due to the imitation, conscious or unconscious, of forms found in nature; according to the second hypothesis, form has its own significance, that is to say, corresponds to some inner psychic necessity, and is expressive of this feeling. Such feeling is not necessarily indeterminate; on the contrary, it is often a desire for reification, clarification, precision, order.

Let us now look a little more closely at some of the first human artifacts, and let us take, for the sake of contrast, a solid cutting form, such as the axe-head (*Plate 31*), and a hollow containing form, such as the clay vessel (*Plate 36*).

The first stages in the formal development of the axe-head were obviously pragmatic – a selection of the stone for size and compactness, for striking-power consistent with handiness. Important, too, at a later stage of development, was an ovoid shape that permitted the attachment of the head to a shaft by means of thongs. But once this basic form had been standardized by a process of trial and correction, then the tool-maker began to concentrate on the cutting power of the axe, and this led to a gradual refinement of the flaking technique, and then to smoothing and polishing by various methods of abrasion. What was finally evolved, allowing for differences due to the nature of the material, was a shape essentially the same as the axe of civilized man (*Plate 32*). In all tool design there is an optimum point of functional efficiency which determines shape in the terms of the material used. In many of his artifacts – spear and arrow heads, scrapers, blades, as well as axes – man reached this optimum point in the Late or Upper Palaeolithic Period.

Then began the final and most significant stage of formal evolution, which does not take place before the Mesolithic Period or Middle Stone Age, perhaps not before the Neolithic Period: the axe was divorced from its utilitarian function, and further refined to serve as a ritual or ceremonial object (*Plate 32*). At this stage even the original material, which for a practical tool had to be as strong as possible, was sometimes abandoned, and in its place a rare and precious material, such as jadite, was substituted (*Plates 29, 30*). Jadite and nephrite are hard stones, and were undoubtedly used for the making of tools before such tools became ritualistic or ceremonial objects; and stone or bronze tools also became ritualistic or ceremonial objects where jadite and nephrite was scarce or unknown. But scarcity leads to preciousness, to scarcity values, and for this reason we may suppose that where it was available, notably in China, jadite or nephrite was preferred for non-utilitarian objects. In any case, form, having become divorced from function, was free to develop according to new principles or laws – those laws and principles which we now call aesthetic.

Archaeologists may differ in the classification of prehistoric stone implements – there is naturally a large intermediate group which may be either refined functional forms or free aesthetic forms, but no archaeologist will question this general outline of the development. It is not essential, however, to find a ritualistic justification for every aesthetic form; there are arrow-heads, for example, of extraordinary grace and refinement, which were certainly weapons of the chase, and in no sense ritualistic. It must be admitted that 'a purely aesthetic principle of elegance' can be combined with, and be indistinguishable from, a purely utilitarian principle of efficiency. Symmetry, for example, an aesthetic quality when man is conscious of it, was undoubtedly at first a technical necessity: an asymmetrical arrow-head would not fly straight. The problem is to determine at what point elegance ceases to be utilitarian, at what point form is divorced from function.

The ceremonial axe, which has its origins in the Late Stone Age, is highly elaborated in the Bronze Age and then persists throughout most cultures down to the Middle Ages in Europe. This artifact, in its refined stages of development, became a symbolic form. Magnificent bronze axes, which can scarcely have been real weapons, were common in ancient China. Dr Gunnar Andersson states that the axe was one of the symbols of fertility in the Neolithic period, and compares to it the hammer which Tori laid on the knees of the bride.[4] Jade axe-heads of the Chou period were certainly cult objects. In the Minoan civilization the double-bladed axe (the *labyris*) was associated with whatever cult was practised in the labyrinth (to which it gave its name). Placed within a circle (for example, between the curved horns of an ox) it becomes a mandala. In later civilizations we find the axe used as a symbol of authority in, for example, the Roman *fasces*, and its symbolic function persists in the ceremonial halberds of the Medieval and Renaissance pageants. Parallels can be found in Mexican and African cultures. But it is not the historical continuity of the form that is of immediate interest, but the nature of the form that guarantees such continuity.

A similar development with even longer continuity can be traced from the Stone Age hammer to the mace (*Plates 33, 34, 35b*) which is still the symbol of royal and parliamentary authority in several countries. Some authorities[5] suggest that the Chinese *pi* (*Plate 35a*), a jade disc varying considerably in size, generally between 10 and 20 cm. in diameter, and pierced in the centre with a circular hole, was derived from the Neolithic mace – a stone mace has been found on a Neolithic site in Mongolia. The *pi* symbolises heaven and was used in sacrificial ceremonies. It was also a token of rank and one of the emblematic objects used in burial rites.

The evolution of the hollow vessel is even more interesting and complicated. The first vessels were small pieces of rock with one surface concave enough to hold a liquid. Use must also have been made of gourds, cocoa-nut shells, fish-shells, and other natural objects; and the progress of cutting and scraping tools must have made possible the hollowing of wood.

With the transition from hunting to agriculture, the possibility of working new materials was discovered, and in particular the plastic virtues of the soil which had become the source of man's basic food, grain. Max Raphael, one of the few archaeologists who has given any thought to the problem of form, in his monograph on prehistoric Egyptian pottery, gives this account of the origins of the clay vessel: 'Man sought unceasingly for new materials, techniques, and ideologies by which to develop his creative abilities in the face of superior natural forces. The alluviated ground, the nature of which remained a mystery to him, produced what he needed by dint of unremitting labour that entailed a number of equally mysterious and unknown changes beyond the control of man.'

'Because of this complex interaction of necessity and creative power', Raphael continues, 'man looked upon the products of this soil, the periodic harvest of barley and wheat that could not be increased at will, with feelings that neither the fruit gatherers nor the hunters had ever experienced – that is, with a desire to store them providentially for future security. Thus with the boom of harvests there was born the need for vessels impervious to moisture and sand, receptacles that could protect the fruits of nature and man's labour from decay.'[6]

The possibility of moulding clay was eventually discovered, and of baking it in the sun or the embers of a fire: 'Experience taught the Neolithic Egyptian that the silt from which the grain grew was pliant and plastic, that the sun dried it and made it serviceable as a container, and that firing made it impervious to water. The man who synthetized these separate experiences invented the clay vessel. And in thereby satisfying one of the most urgent social needs, he raised the spiritual value of the material that not only served the growth of grain but also made possible the preservation of it. Man saw that his entire existence depended upon a substance whose origin and nature he did not understand and which he could not produce himself.'[7]

But the Neolithic Egyptian could give form to this mysterious substance. The first vessels were round semi-spherical bowls (*Plate 36*), but the nature of the material inspired variations from the beginning – bowls with low walls became platters, bowls with high walls became beakers and grain urns. Then came the desire to cover the bowl, for better containment of the liquid, for better protection from flies, and to mould its shape for better pouring or for carrying – each need calling forth an adaptation of the prototype. And again the process of refinement of the basic utilitarian shape set in, and here one must suppose that certain affinities with the shape of the human body had an unconscious influence. Symmetry was imposed by the need for balance, and for the same reason a foot or base was differentiated. The need to lift and transport the larger vessels led to the addition of lugs or handles, but always at some point in the evolution of the utilitarian shape, utility is exceeded. The form is refined for its own sake, or for the sake of a function that is no longer strictly utilitarian. The vessel may be used for libations, for holding grain or the ashes of the dead; and such ritualistic functions can justify refinements not required for normal use. What is essential to note is that at some point in this process of formal evolution the form responds not only to a utilitarian purpose, but also to a spiritual need.

The important point to realize is that (again in Max Raphael's words) 'the fashioning of clay went beyond gratification of physical needs'. And Raphael makes the further subtle point that 'this development was favoured by the fact (erroneously regarded by many writers as a limitation) that the human hand could produce the synthesis between utilitarian and spiritual purposefulness without resort to any tool'.

We must still ask by what forces, and under what guiding will, did the utilitarian shapes of the first clay vessels become the refined forms of later cultures? Max Raphael, who was a dialectical materialist by philosophical conviction, believed that the forces were economic – new needs, often imported by invading races who transformed the old conditions of life.

Max Raphael argues that when the material conditions change, man's emotional reactions change, among these his aesthetic reactions. The old forms no longer satisfy the new feelings: they must be modified to correspond to an inner necessity, a will to form which is an emotional reaction to life as a whole – 'the totality of all interacting objective conditions', as he calls it. This seems to imply that there was an evolving consciousness of form as such. 'When Neolithic man, motivated perhaps by the practical purpose of achieving greater imperviousness to liquids, combined polishing with painting and applied both to a form he had created (*Plate 37*), his consciousness of freedom was increased. The new means of representation changed the impression produced by the pot, and man consequently gained insight regarding the difference between the actual nature and the effect of a given form. Formerly, when the prehistoric artist for the first time applied mathematics to matter, the effect was only an outward adjustment – the weight of the material, despite its smoothness, still opposed the abstraction of mathematics. Now, when polished colour concealed the material from the eye, the mind began to play with the impression of gravitational pull and tried to eliminate it. This tendency was heightened by the fact that the material was actually reduced to a fairly thin layer. In the much-admired thinness of Badarian pottery we are confronted not only with virtuosity (which surely must have had a high market value), not only with the purely aesthetic principle of elegance, but with a general ideological force that attempted to play with the opposition between matter and spirit, that is, endeavoured to stress or to eliminate this opposition by dematerializing the material and materializing the immaterial.'[8]

Here we have a formula for the power that transforms a utilitarian shape into a work of art – an ideological power that *plays* with the opposition between spirit and matter and endeavours to eliminate this opposition. Before we consider the adequacy of this formula, which might be illustrated even more strikingly by tracing the evolution of the bronze vessel in Neolithic China, let us glance at the origins of form in pictorial art.

We have established three stages in the development of the shape of objects of utility – namely (1) discovery of the functional form, (2) refinement of the functional form to its maximum efficiency, and (3) refinement of the functional form in the direction of free or symbolic form. To suppose *a priori* that pictorial art, the art of representing images, underwent similar stages of development would perhaps be unwarranted. It is, of course, just possible that the first depictions of animals had a utilitarian purpose – a tally system for huntings or killings – but before the art of drawing could reach the value of a representational symbol, there must have been a long process of development, upward from aimless scratching or scribbling in sand or on the damp clayey walls of the caves. Scribbles and the outlined silhouettes of hands have survived in various palaeolithic sites, and though there is no stratographical evidence to constitute an evolutionary development from aimless scribbling to the representational image or schema, the analogy of the similar development of pictorial representation in the drawings of children is perhaps admissible. But this is not the random activity ending in an accidental discovery of resemblances that a superficial observation might lead one to suppose it to be. Patient analysis of the scribbling activity in children, such as that conducted by Mrs Rhoda Kellogg among infants in San Francisco, shows that there is a progressive discovery of basic forms – the circle, the cross, the square, and so on – all tending towards a synthetic form which is our old friend, the mandala – a circle divided into four sections. This mandala constitutes a basic schema from which images are developed by the process already mentioned which Professor Gombrich has called 'making and matching'[9] – that is to say, the schema is gradually modified in the direction of the retinal image, until a convincing approximation is achieved. On this hypothesis it can be maintained that 'what the artist knows' (the schema) is gradually modified by 'what the artist sees' (the illusion of reality) and that this process accounts for all variations of style in the history of representational art.

From this point of view chance rock formations or protuberances on the wall of the cave might have served as schemas for Palaeolithic man, but this is a phenomenon that occurs most frequently at the peak of Franco-Cantabrian art. Paolo Graziosi, in the latest and most comprehensive survey of Palaeolithic art, comes to the conclusion that 'nothing so far proves that fortuitous realism acted as a dominant creative impulse in the earliest forms

33. *Votive hammer-head dedicated to the god Nergal. Babylon, c.2500 BC*

34. *Mace-head dedicated to the god Mes-lam-Ta-E-A. Babylon, c.2250 BC*

35a. Disc (pi.) Chinese, Neolithic period

35b. Mace. Chinese, Neolithic period

36. *Pottery vessel.*
Egypt, Badarian period

37. *Redware vase.*
Egypt, Amratian period

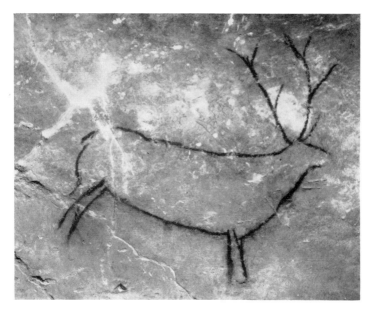

38. *Stag in outline.* *Wall painting from Las Chimeneas, Puente Viesgo*

39. *Two Bison.* *Wall painting from Lascaux*

of art' – on the contrary 'it flourished especially in those who had attained a high degree of sensitivity in form and volume, and a remarkable mastery of technical skills'.[10]

It is reasonable to suppose, however, that casual scratches and scribbles may have suggested a mental schema to which the deliberate drawing was then matched – or equally probably, there may have been a gradual attempt to match the scribble to the eidetic image. But the more successful the attempt, the less interesting it becomes from a formal point of view: the reproduction of an eidetic image, however life-like, is not necessarily a work of art. It is an illustration and only becomes a work of art if there is an intention to compose or arrange the image in a significant form. The exact illustration of a reindeer or a rhinoceros corresponds to the tool of maximum efficiency. To constitute an artistic form the illustration must be carried beyond this utilitarian stage towards a conception of pure form. Or, to put the same thought in another way: the exact representation of an animal is a reproduction of natural form; we are concerned with artifacts, which are forms contrived by the human imagination.

It has been suggested by some archaeologists that certain of the drawings of animals at Altamira were deliberately composed in this manner: they have 'style' as well as 'exactitude'. But a categorical distinction must be made between 'style' and 'form'. Style corresponds to vitality, to kinetic qualities; form to beauty, to static qualities. Style is human, and limited to human artifacts; form is universal, and exists only when human artifacts correspond to mathematical laws. In general we may say that the Palaeolithic artist achieved style but was not aware of form.

We still lack, however, a convincing explanation of why, so early in human development, the approximation of image to reality should have been achieved with such efficiency, though only in one category – the representation of animals. That explanation, it seems to me, must be sought in the social structure that conditioned the production of the images – that is to say, in the very precise requirements of the magical practices of Palaeolithic man. I have suggested also that it would be legitimate to suppose, at this early stage of human development, a constitutional acuteness of imagery in the human brain – that is to say, a prevailing *eidetic* imagery such as children and certain animals may possess. But if children possess such images, why do they not also produce drawings of similar realistic accuracy? I think one can say: because they have no compelling motive such as the fear and hunger that through a long period of development drove prehistoric man to the institution and elaboration of sympathetic magic.

It is obvious that between any preliminary scribbling stage in the development of prehistoric representational art and the attainment of realistic imagery there once more intervened a will, and though in this case the will did not work upon a utilitarian shape, a tool, it nevertheless seized on a given form – the basic scribble form – and began to transform it with some ulterior intention. We must suppose that the basic form – the mandala – had been achieved by an unconscious will – we may, if we wish to remain materialistic up to this point, suppose that it is no more than a perceptual process that automatically, by reason of perceptual ease and balance, achieves the good *Gestalt*. But the modification of the basic form then proceeds by an equally perceptual process of making and matching to a point where the illusion of realism is achieved. This stage we may regard as equivalent to the elaboration of the perfectly functional tool – the realistic image is a tool required by sympathetic magic. But then, perhaps in some of the Palaeolithic drawings at Altamira, but more obviously in the carved amulets of the female figure such as the Venuses of Lespugue (France) and Dolní Vestoniče (Mikulov District of Moravia) formalization approaches to abstraction. There intervenes a will to form that carries the image beyond its utilitarian function and beyond even its stylistic vitality, to constitute once again *free* or *symbolic form*. What takes place is an elaboration of the realistic or utilitarian image, and a gradual substitution, for this image, of a shape that has a power of attraction, and of satisfaction, that proceeds from the shape itself and not from its perceptual or representational function.[11]

It would seem, therefore, that in whatever direction we investigate the origins of form, we see the emergence of an independent will-to-form, which usually begins to manifest itself when the functional efficiency of the form has reached its optimum point of development and has then become stabilized. We still have no adequate conception of the causation of this will, nor indeed of its teleological justification. Is it merely, as some aestheticians have supposed, a playful impulse to elegant variation; or can it possess a motivation in terms of man's biological evolution? I assume that within the term 'biological evolution', we must be prepared to include the development of those faculties by means of which man achieves a mental, that is to say, a spiritual, adjustment to the mystery of his existential situation – a means of answering what Heidegger has called the fundamental question: why is there anything at all, rather than nothing; and how do we establish an apprehensible form for what *is* – how do we establish being? In other words, more appropriate to our immediate concern: why are the forms established by the artist of universal significance?

2

Form, as Heidegger has recognized, belongs to the very essence of being. Being (*Sein*) is that which achieves a limit for itself. 'That which places itself in its limit, completing itself, and so stands, has form, *morphē*. Form, as the Greeks understood it, derives its essence from an emerging placing-itself-in-the-limit.'[12]

Such is the form that we have seen emerging at the dawn of human history: such is the formative capacity that distinguishes *homo sapiens* from *homo faber*. For the forms of *homo faber*, the practical and functional tools of the first stages of human development, did not reach a limit of being (*Ständigkeit*), but merely expressed a restless busy-ness. It was not until form had reached the limit of efficiency or usefulness that it became form-in-itself, permanent being.

It then became the *logos*. According to Heidegger the basic meaning of *logos* is gathering and togetherness, and in his words, 'gathering is never a mere driving together and heaping-up. It maintains in a common bond the conflicting and that which tends apart. It does not let them fall into haphazard dispersion. In thus maintaining a bond, the *logos* has the character of permeating power, of *physis*. It does not let what it holds in its power dissolve into an empty freedom from opposition, but by uniting the opposites maintains the full sharpness of their tension.'[13]

Heidegger derives this meaning of *logos* from Heraclitus, and interprets one of the fragments in the Diels-Kranz arrangement (the first) as an identification of *physis* and *logos*. In what I believe to be a very faithful translation of this obscure fragment, it reads: 'Although this Logos is eternally valid, yet men are unable to understand it – not only before hearing it, but even after they heard it for the first time. That is to say, although all things come to pass in accordance with this Logos, men seem to be quite without any experience of it – at least if they are judged in the light of such words and deeds as I am here setting forth. My own method is to distinguish each thing according to its nature, and to specify how it behaves; other men, on the contrary, are as forgetful and heedless in their waking moments of what is going on around and within them as they are during sleep.'[14] In another fragment (the eighth) Heraclitus says: 'Opposites move back and forth, the one to the other; from out of themselves they gather themselves', or, to quote another translation: 'Opposition brings concord. Out of discord comes the fairest harmony.' Heidegger interprets this fragment in the sense that the conflict of opposites is a gathering, rooted in togetherness, it is *logos*. From his identification of *logos* with *physis* Heidegger passes to beauty, for what the Greeks meant by beauty was restraint. '*Art is disclosure of the being of the essent.*' 'The being of the essent is the supreme radiance, i.e. the greatest beauty, that which is most permanent in itself. . . . For us moderns, on the contrary, the beautiful is what reposes and relaxes; it is intended for enjoyment and art is a matter for pastry cooks.'[15] For the Greeks beauty was the radiance of what is complete and harmonious, of what is self-contained and original. The work of art is a disclosure of being, the establishment of a pristine relation to *physis*, the realm of things, to nature, to being itself. But, as Heidegger makes so beautifully clear, 'the Greeks did not learn what *physis* is through natural phenomena, but the other way round: it was through a fundamental poetic and intellectual experience of being that they discovered what they had to call *physis*. It was this discovery that enabled them to gain a glimpse into nature in the restricted sense. Hence *physis* originally encompassed heaven as well as earth, the stone as well as the plant, the animal as well as the man, and it encompassed human history as a work of men and gods; and ultimately and first of all, it meant the gods themselves as subordinated to destiny. *Physis* means the power that emerges and the enduring realm under its sway. This power of emerging and enduring includes "becoming" as well as "being" in the restricted sense of inert duration. *Physis* is the process of a-rising, of emerging from the hidden, whereby the hidden is first made to stand.'[16]

But what emerges is a form, *morphē*, and what emerges has form by virtue of its togetherness, it inner relatedness, its harmony. It is usually said that the Greeks had no word for art, and the word *technē* is substituted; but the Greeks had no word for art because they did not conceive it as separate from the apprehension of reality, the establishment of being, from physics and metaphysics. *Technē*, says Heidegger, was neither art nor technology, but a knowledge, the ability to plan and organize freely, to master institutions, and he refers us to Plato's *Phaedrus* in justification. '*Technē* is creating, building in the sense of a deliberate producing'; it is the ability to invent the efficient tool, but not the free form. But elsewhere Heidegger redefines *technē* as knowledge in the authentic sense, not as mere observation concerning previously unknown data, but as the actual doing which results in the production of objects,[17] 'the initial and persistent looking out beyond what is given at any time'. Art can then be identified with *technē* because art 'is what most immediately brings being (i.e. the appearing that stands there in itself) to stand, stabilizes it into something present (the work). The work of art is a work not primarily because it is wrought (*gewirkt*), made (we have seen that the tool satisfies these conditions), but because it brings about (*er-wirkt*) being in an essent; it brings about the phenomenon in which the emerging power, *physis*, comes to shine (*scheinen*). It is through the work of art as essent being that everything else that appears and is to be found is first confirmed and made accessible, explicable, and understandable as being or not being.'[18]

Art, therefore, may be regarded as 'the ability, pure and simple, to accomplish, to put-into-the-work (*ins-Werk-setzen*), as *technē*.' Such a manifesting realization of being is knowledge, and art is *technē* in this sense: as knowledge, not because it involves 'technical' skill, tools, materials.

This distinction of Heidegger's seems to be beautifully illustrated by the early evolution of artifacts as I have described it. *Technē* in the sense of skill will account for the form of the artifact as a tool designed for practical needs; but *technē* in the sense of making and manifesting brings about a form that stands there in itself, disassociated from its practical function, a configuration disclosing itself as the being of the essent.

In reading Heidegger's interpretation of the early Greek philosophy one is inevitably reminded of a philosophy that was contemporary with it, the Chinese, and there one finds an attempt to explain the establishment of being which can be closely related to early Greek thought. It is beyond my powers to attempt a correlation of the Greek and the Chinese cosmologies, but I can perhaps indicate some analogies. There is the same awareness of Being and Non-being, and of the mystery of the emergence of form from a primordial chaos. According to the *Huai-nan-Tzu*, a second century B.C. miscellaneous compilation of all schools of thought which summarizes earlier philosophic writings, two contrary principles, the *yin* and the *yang*, gradually emerged from a complex and universal energy, and by uniting, these contrary principles constituted the first harmonious forms. To quote from Derk Bodde's translation of the *Huai-nan-Tzu*:

'When Heaven and Earth did not yet have form, there was a state of amorphous formlessness. Therefore this is termed the Great Beginning (*t'ai shih*). This Great Beginning produced an empty extensiveness, and this empty extensiveness produces the cosmos. The cosmos produced the primal fluid (*yüan ch'i*), which had its limits. That which was clear and light collected to form Heaven. That which was heavy and turbid congealed to form Earth. The union of the clear and the light was especially easy, whereas the congealing of the heavy and the turbid was particularly difficult, so that Heaven was formed first and Earth afterward.

'The essences of Heaven and Earth formed the *yin* and the *yang*, and the concentrated essences of the *yin* and the *yang* formed the four seasons. The scattered essences of the four seasons formed the myriad things. The hot force of *yang*, being accumulated for a long time, produced fire, and the essence of fire formed the sun. The cold force of *yin*, being accumulated for a long time, produced water, and the essence of water formed the moon. The refined essence of the excess fluid of the sun and moon formed the stars and planets. Heaven received unto itself the sun, moon, stars and planets, while Earth received water, rivers, soil and dust.'[19]

This process of formation, of a gathering of opposites, a *logos*, remains on the cosmological level in Chinese thought, but the process does not end with water, rivers, soil and dust, but is extended by analogy to living plants and animals, and finally to the human race and its artifacts. The work of art is conceived as a symbol of cosmic units, as a reification of the concentrated essences of the *yin* and the *yang*.

A more significant analogy, perhaps, for our purpose is the evolution of the trigrams used in the process of divination as practised in the *I Ching*. According to early Chinese historians, divination was originally made by means of the tortoise shell, which was heated with fire by the diviner, who then interpreted the cracks which appeared on its surface. The eight trigrams, and the sixty-four hexagrams derived from these by combining any two into diagrams of six lines each, were intended as a formal substitute for the chaos of lines that appeared on the heated tortoise shell, and were probably introduced at about the same time that form began to emerge as a conscious entity in the artifacts of the Chinese – the period of the Five Emperors,[20] or the Yang-Shao period as it is now usually called after the site of one of the Neolithic villages of about 3000 to 2500 B.C. discovered by Dr J.Gunnar Andersson.[21] I am not suggesting that the parallel between the discovery of pure form in such artifacts as the axe-head or the adze and the invention of the trigrams is an exact one, but we may discount the legend that the trigrams were actually invented by Fu Hsi (according to another legend he found them on the back of a dragon-horse that suddenly rose from the waters of the Yellow River). It is more probable that the legends were invented to explain the gradual evolution of formal shapes from the intricate cracks on the heated tortoise shells.

It should then be observed that the form of each trigram has a sign value, or symbolic significance. The signs consist of the eight possible combinations of broken and unbroken lines in threes, and it is said that the unbroken line represents the male principle, the broken line the female principle (equally they may represent 'the hot force of *yang*' and 'the cold force of *yin*'). Wilhelm, in his edition of the *I Ching*,[22] classifies the various attributes, images and family relationships that the eight trigrams symbolize: the details are not significant for our present purpose, but only the fact that a formal arrangement, a *Gestalt*, has become endowed with a sign value, or with symbolical significance. The symbols may seem fairly obvious (and should therefore more correctly be called signs) – a combination of three unbroken lines signifies the creative, the strong, heaven, and father; whereas a combination of three broken lines signifies the receptive, the yielding, earth and mother, but the symbolism becomes less obvious in the more intricate combinations, and very obscure when the eight trigrams are combined with one another to make sixty-four symbols.

Why should form have symbolic significance? – that is the question to which we must finally address ourselves, for we may assume that pure or artistic form would never have been separated from the utilitarian shape unless the mind of man had suddenly perceived a non-utilitarian significance in the shape, a manifesting realization of being.

There are three possibilities:

(1) That a symbolic function developed from the utilitarian function – e.g. the axe used in sacrifices acquired by association a ritual significance in addition to its utilitarian purpose, and its form was on that account gradually refined.

(2) That a symbolic value was attached to a form because it resembled a natural object – e.g. the unbroken line is the creative male organ, the broken line the receptive female organ.

(3) That the form itself became significant because it acquired harmonic proportions. We must on this supposition ask further why harmony should be significant.

I think we can dismiss the second of these possibilities for the semantic reason already given: a form that has significance because it resembles another object is not a symbol, but a sign. A symbol is only a symbol in so far as it signifies an unknown, or not otherwise expressible, perception or feeling.

We are therefore left with two values that may be symbolized in a created form: one of perception and sensation, the other of intuition and feeling. What is evident to perception and sensation is the radiance of being; what is evident to intuition and feeling is the gathering-together-in-itself, the formal restraint.

Consciousness itself is formal: not so much form-giving as form-receiving. That is to say, we understand experience in so far as it is presented to consciousness as form. 'From the very first, so to speak, consciousness is a symbolizing activity. Hence one never finds in it anything barely "given" without meaning and reference beyond itself. There is no content that is not construed according to some form.'[23] That was the great affirmation that Kant made in his *Critique of Pure Reason*, and it has never been convincingly disproved. On the contrary, it has been developed in our time into an all-embracing philosophy of form by the genius of Ernst Cassirer, on whom I shall rely for my concluding observations on this problem.

There was form before there was human consciousness of form; the universe itself, the *yin* and the *yang* that emerged out of primal chaos and formed concentrated essences. Human consciousness began with the forms of perception, and human intelligence and spirituality with the representation of form. Man's freedom and his culture begins with a *will* to form. Language, the sustaining medium of his imagination, is a formal creation. Art itself is a will to form, and not merely an involuntary or instinctive reaction. 'The moment of *purposiveness* is necessary for linguistic and artistic expression. In every act of speech and in every artistic creation we find a definite teleological function.'[24] Or, as Cassirer says in another place: 'The artistic eye is not a passive eye that receives and registers the impression of things. It is a constructive eye, and it is only by constructive acts that we discover the beauty of natural things. The sense of beauty is the susceptibility to the dynamic life of forms, and this life cannot be apprehended except by a corresponding dynamic process in ourselves.'[25]

Applying this observation to the first human artifacts that revealed artistic form, we must still ask: how did that susceptibility to the dynamic life of forms come into being?

We can only grope for an answer to this question. We know that the concept of abstract space, for example, was not discovered before the time of Democritus (460 to 360 B.C.) – it was one of the distinctive achievements of Greek thought. We cannot assume that the human beings who first discovered beauty in the Neolithic age had any abstract conceptions, of space, or proportion, or harmony. Theirs was an unreflective, sensational experience. If therefore form became significant for Neolithic man, it was an act of perception and not of intelligence. In so far as Neolithic man was purposive in giving an artistic form to his artifacts, the purpose must have been a progressive approximation towards a sense of form derived from his general experience. That is to say, man must have gradually acquired from his material environment a conditioned response to those physical properties of symmetry and harmonic proportion which his senses received from the observed form of his own body, the forms of animals and plants, the rhythm of day and night, and so on. Since form is prior to human experience, we can legitimately assume that the consciousness of form was received from the natural environment of man, and then spontaneously matched in his artifacts. But it was the form that was matched, not the appearance, and it was the form that was symbolic.

The purpose of such symbolic forms, we may assume with Heidegger and Cassirer, was to disclose meaning, to create the tools of discourse. 'Since every particular content of consciousness is situated in a network of diverse relations', Cassirer observes, 'by virtue of which its simple existence and self-representation contain *reference* to other and still other contents, there can and must be certain formations of consciousness in which the pure form of reference is, as it were, sensuously embodied. From this follows the characteristic twofold nature of these formations: their bond with sensibility, which however contains within it a freedom from sensibility. In every linguistic "sign", in every mythical or artistic "image", a spiritual content, which intrinsically points beyond the whole sensory sphere, is translated into the form of the sensuous, into something visible, audible, or tangible. An independent mode of configuration appears, a specific activity of consciousness, which is differentiated from any datum of immediate sensation or perception, but makes use of these data as vehicles, as means of expression.'[26]

That passage from Cassirer's great work contains, it seems to me, in concentrated essence the answer to our question. The transition from a refined but still utilitarian form, produced under necessity, is effected at the cross-roads of consciousness, where forms meet and mingle; and at this encounter forms first acquire at once their freedom and their expressive function. At this moment 'consciousness *creates* definite concrete sensory contents as an expression for definite complexes of meaning. And because these contents which consciousness creates are entirely in its power, it can, through them, freely "evoke" all those meanings at any time.' In other words, language and art acquire their symbolic functions: a symbolic discourse, divorced from material necessity, then becomes possible.

We cannot reconstruct or even imagine that 'moment' in prehistory when form first disclosed being, when man for the first time stabilized being into the concreteness of a work of art. One might as well ask at what 'moment' was consciousness born in the human race. But my object in this essay has been to show that the origins of form in art are also the origins of *logos*, of knowledge of being, of reality. Art, in so far as it has retained its primary function and not become 'a matter for pastry cooks', has throughout history always been such a mode of revelation, of establishment, of naming. This was all said succinctly, in one line of verse, by Hölderlin:

Was bleibet aber, stiften die Dichter

What endures is established by poets; that is to say, man achieves being and identity by virtue of his creative activity, his will to form.

IV

Informality

The discussion of the problem of form in art so far undertaken assumes a rather simple distinction between form and the distortion of form, between harmony and disharmony, between beauty and ugliness. There is, however, a further distinction to be made between form itself as an order established by human sensibility amidst the apparent chaos of visual phenomena, and the direct or mimetic representation of those same phenomena in their actuality. This, which is a distinction evident enough from an objective consideration of the history of art, has only in our own time become an inescapable choice for the artist.

I know of only one philosopher of art who has treated this problem in all its semantic and logical aspects – the late Richard Bernheimer in his book *The Nature of Representation*.[1] The problem has also been treated with great erudition by Professor E. H. Gombrich in *Art and Illusion: A study in the Psychology of Pictorial Representation*,[2] but I feel that Professor Gombrich fails to account for the profound significance of man's invented forms, as distinct from representational forms. As one critic noted: 'His is a book of exposure rather than of revelation. Nowhere does it deal with the core of artistic representation, namely, with what takes place when an artist, or period of art, possessed by a vital conception of human existence, rallies all available tools and resources to invent a profoundly significant visual form.'[3]

Bernheimer neglects no aspect of the problem, and though he is no partisan of abstraction, he does realize that 'It would seem likely, even without detailed analysis, that a symbol – any symbol – functions by virtue of an inner process more recondite and more penetrating than that which governs our understanding of simple likeness. Theories of representation which overlook this disparity have little chance of reflecting more than a mere fraction of the truth'.[4]

Professor Bernheimer reviews all existing theories of representation, a detailed exposition which I do not intend to summarize. He does not, however, pay particular attention to that aspect of form which I now propose to discuss, irregular form, or informality. In so far as irregular forms have a 'sign function', they are included in the distinction he makes between representation and sign function, and in particular they would be included in the function which Professor Bernheimer calls 'substitution'. He argues that the current identification of representation with sign function is illegitimate – 'that while the two modes of apprehension overlap, the field of representation is wider than the area which it shares with its sister function, comprising phenomena which no theory of semantics, however constituted, can ever claim for itself; that representation has an inner structure of its own, akin to but by no means identical with that possessed by various categories of signs; and finally that the function most akin to representation is not, as semanticists suppose, that of signification, but the much neglected and little known one of substitution'.[5]

Substitution, says Bernheimer, is a natural function and representation a mental one. I am not sure of the meaning of 'natural' in this context, but I hope that it would include mental processes that are instinctive, or, as we now say, unconscious. For there does undoubtedly take place in art a mode of substitution that is based on the perception of biologically relevant (and therefore 'natural') shapes. In a book of fundamental importance for the study of our subject[6] Anton Ehrenzweig advanced a theory of unconscious perception that succeeded in carrying out in the sphere of art an intention once expressed by William James as 'the reinstatement of the vague to its proper place in mental life'. It would be difficult to summarize this theory, but it establishes a distinction between two principles of perception, one 'the abstract gestalt principle which guides our surface perception towards "good" gestalt, i.e. towards precise, compact, coherent, aesthetically "good" shapes', and a second principle of perception 'which guides surface perception towards the biologically relevant thing shapes' (that is, shapes that are gestalt-free). For the first time Mr Ehrenzweig gave a convincing psychological explanation for the mysterious fact that many of our artistic experiences are concerned with 'the inarticulate form elements hidden in the unconscious structure of the work of art or – what comes to the same thing – with the unconscious structure of the perception processes by which we actively create or passively enjoy these unconscious form elements'.

In discussing the origins of form in art (Chapter III) I may have given the impression that the artistic impulse is exclusively concerned with the desire to achieve the 'good' gestalt, the precise, coherent and compact form, or, alternatively, with that distortion of form we call ugliness. If so I must now correct that impression, for it is based on a distinction between realism and utilitarianism that perhaps does not exist, either historically or theoretically. I used the evolution of the artifact, the utilitarian object, as a basis for my theory of the origins of form. We may assume that concurrently, at least for the period during which form evolved towards the aesthetic gestalt, prehistoric man was developing his ability to project a realistic (mimetic) image, especially the images demanded for the efficacy of his magical or ritualistic practices. If the stratographical evidence permits the assumption that the making of tools and the painting of mimetic representations of animals went on side by side, we must then ask whether the formative capacities involved in these two distinct activities were inspired by different motives.

This question is not of merely theoretical or historical signi-cance. I intend to show that the motivations involved persist to the present day and account for some of the contradictions of contemporary art.

What is significant, if our generalizations about prehistoric art are true, is that the utilitarian object – the axe, the spear-head, the mace, etc. – was only redeemed from its strictly utilitarian function in order to become a cult object. That is to say, it was redeemed from its spiritual insignificance and given symbolic significance at the same time that its form was refined and given those characteristics that distinguish a work of art. Such characteristics from the beginning were complex: measurable characteristics such as harmonic proportion, indefinite characteristics such as vitality.

The whole of this hypothesis, it will be seen, assumes the pre-existence of a formless chaos or shapelessness out of which form gradually emerges and is endowed, whether consciously or unconsciously, with significance. But can we assume that chaos itself, the original formlessness or limitlessness of being, is without positive significance of any kind? We have seen that the Unknown is the source of terror and *Angst* – in other words, that it acts upon human sensibility in a most powerful though incoherent manner: why do we exclude the possibility that chaos and dark nothingness were from the beginning the source of emotions of an aesthetic kind? In other words, must we logically associate art with an emergent consciousness of form? Might there not have been, from the beginning of human consciousness, such a thing as an awareness of the aesthetic significance of informal objects?

In Chapter II I discussed the concept of the sublime, as it originated with Longinus and was subsequently developed by eighteenth-century philosophers like Burke. The significance of this concept is that it allows aesthetic value to formless dimensions, to what Burke called 'the artificial infinite'. The word 'artificial' is important in this connection, for Burke held that in so far as the formless or the infinite was experienced directly, the reaction of the spectator was merely fearsome; in order to inspire 'delight', such emotional states had to be represented, or, as the modern aesthetician would say, 'distanced'. We enjoy the representation of scenes of terror because we enjoy the discovery that we are experiencing them vicariously.

What is formless, however, is not necessarily infinite or terrifyingly indefinite; nor is the infinite necessarily formless. It is doubtful if it is conceivable apart from finite forms – Ruskin once suggested that the effect of infinity is achieved in a painting by 'no more than such a mere luminous distant point as may give to the feelings a species of escape from all the finite objects about them'. He gives as an example 'a subdued window light, seen in the opening between two columns', which gives this kind of dimension to Rembrandt's etching of *The Presentation of Christ in the Temple*.[7] We avoid the issue if we conceive the formless as without expressible definition. Clouds, for example, are informal, but they are not formless. If a cumulus cloud is isolated in a blue sky, it has a form that stands out from its environment of infinite space. Many other natural phenomena, such as forests, lichens and fungi, the configuration of islands and lakes, have the same irregular but limiting outlines, and if we become conscious of such a distinct area, we recognize its informal limits, and in becoming aware of the uniqueness of these limits, respond with feelings of delight that are properly called aesthetic.

Such feelings in relation to irregular forms cannot logically be denied to prehistoric man, but this fact is not inconsistent with a theory of the origin of form in art in which the first recognition of form-in-itself, whether that form be natural or the result of technical skills, was also that moment in the evolution of human consciousness when form first acquired symbolic value. That is to say, aesthetic form and symbolic form originated at the same time. Further, form could not be isolated, for recognition, without at the same time requiring a recognition of the informal. The consciousness of formality and consciousness of informality developed simultaneously; indeed from an evolutionary point of view there could be no essential difference between the first recognition of form in nature and the first recognition of form in artifacts, and a consequent awareness of the absence of form, or informality-as-such. It is the recognition of form, or, as Heidegger would say, of an essence attached to that-which-has-limits and has thereby acquired permanent being, which constitutes the original aesthetic event.

The distinction we must make, from a logical point of view, is that between the existence of form and the recognition of form. Forms exist in nature that are the product of natural forces; and some of these forms were thought by primitive man to possess magical or spiritual properties. The forms made by man became works of art because they too were thought to possess magical or spiritual properties. The first works of art (the French *objets d'art* is a better term) were works of art in virtue of their form, whether such form was natural or artificial. It is the form, in all its concreteness, in all its *object-ness*, that discloses being. The work of art is a work of limitation, of concentration, *eine Dichtung*, as the German language indicates.

This is not to deny that a superior value, that is to say, a human value, attaches to the work of art, whether natural (the *objet trouvé* of the Surrealists) or artificial. Selectivity is in itself a form of creativity, but if mankind had had to wait for arbitrary and impersonal forces to disclose being, the evolution of consciousness and intelligence would have been a much slower process – indeed, it is doubtful if man would have emerged from the stage of *homo faber*. What matters, in this process, is the disclosure to consciousness of forms that are complete in themselves, and that because of their completeness, can be endowed with significance, with logos in Heidegger's meaning of that word.

These speculations have an obvious application to the art of our own time, which in great part has adopted informality as the specific aim of creative activity. This characteristic of contemporary art might be easier to understand if we could establish the possible awareness of informality as such in the prehistoric period. By informality-as-such I mean, for example, the conscious need to give to the feelings 'a species of escape' from finite objects. In this sense informality is equivalent to infinity. Was prehistoric man conscious of infinity?

It will be said that we have no means of knowing, but we have the right to interpret the evidence in accordance with our general principles, and there is no doubt that prehistoric man had an impulse closely related to the desire to escape from the finitude of all finite objects – I mean the will to abstraction. Siegfried Giedion, in his great work on the beginnings of art, asserts that 'Abstraction runs through the whole of primeval art. In the Aurignacian and Magdalenian periods we find easily recognizable representations of animals together with enigmatic symbols which had no counterpart in the visible world; they crop up over a very wide range but perhaps most strikingly in the great oval hall of Lascaux and in the painted ceiling of Altamira, where bison are placed next to enormous red abstract symbols.

'Art, indeed, began with abstraction'.[8]

There are various types and degrees of abstraction, but there is no doubt that among the types present in primeval art is a type which uses shapes and forms that are nonexistent in nature and that become endowed with symbolic meaning known only to the initiated.[9] Giedion has no hesitation in describing this type of abstraction as 'symbolic', and by symbolization he means 'Neanderthal man's first attempts at a spiritual organization transcending simple materials and a utilitarian existence'. Some of these symbols are straightforward, easily to be interpreted as ritual objects connected with fertility rites, for example, but others are more complex and mysterious. Giedion suggests that such abstract symbols 'arose from the need to give perceptible form to the imperceptible. Symbolization emerged as soon as man had to express the disquieting and intangible relation between life and death. . . .'[10]

I am not for the moment concerned with the purpose of these symbols, but with their forms, or rather with their informality, and above all with the informality of their grouping on the surface of the rock. It may be possible to derive some of the abstract symbols from naturalistic prototypes, but since abstract symbols occur in association with contemporary animal drawings of great fidelity to appearances, there is no doubt that a will to abstraction existed alongside a will to representation. It has recently been maintained by Annette Laming that the association of realistic animals and abstract symbols is not fortuitious – 'the paintings on the walls of the caverns are no fortuitious compositions. They are to be regarded as deliberately planned and arranged designs.'[11] It may be that the association of the various objects depicted in a particular cave is deliberate, but from any aesthetic point of view it is difficult to see anything but informality in, for example, the paintings on the ceiling of the cave at Altamira. They may rather be compared to the arbitrary assemblage of votive offerings in a modern shrine. The design is imposed by the space available.

I need not labour this point, for it does not affect my main purpose, which is to suggest that the origins of informal art are distinct from but may be coeval with the origins of formal art. The best of the traditional definitions of art, the scholastic definition of art as clarity of form, will no longer serve our purpose, unless 'form' is interpreted with a freedom far from the scholastic intention. The difficulty has arisen from the habitual confusion of art with beauty, but we are now free from that error. It is doubtful if art can be more closely defined than as 'a kind of spiritual sensibility in contact with matter', which was a definition once offered by Jacques Maritain.[12] That copulation may from time to time give birth to some hopeful monsters, but we must not condemn them to extinction, for on that freedom, and on that perversity, depends the uniting of opposites which is the establishment of being. We have already identified establishment of being with artistic creation. To repeat a saying of Heraclitus: 'Opposition brings concord. Out of discord comes the fairest harmony.' Out of discord comes the work of art.

V

Form in Architecture

The aesthetics of architecture is a large subject, so I shall begin by eliminating those general aspects of the art that are common to other arts – for example, the concept of beauty itself, which the works of the architect may illustrate but cannot in themselves define. I shall also leave out of account all theories of style, for style is a variable element in the history of art due to personal or social factors – 'the constant form', as Meyer Schapiro has defined it, 'in the art of an individual or a group,' – not, therefore, a constant quality of architecture as an art.[1] I do not pretend that one can separate the problem of style from aesthetics, but the aesthetics of a particular art like architecture is determined by what is peculiar to that art, namely, its materials and functions. We find no difficulty in establishing a subject called 'poetics' for the art of poetry, but the only parallel word to describe the art of building, 'tectonics', does not possess the same theoretical connotation: it generally implies structural principles rather than aesthetic values, and is therefore not inclusive enough for my purpose. Tectonics is derived from the Greek word for a carpenter, and the underlying implication (as in all Greek terminology for the arts) is that of a craft. Wisely or unwisely, modern aesthetics has made a categorical distinction between art and craft, and I propose to observe this distinction, and to justify it.

Architectural Association Journal, LXXV, No. 842, May 1960.

I have already discussed in my book on *The Art of Sculpture*[2] the significant fact that in their beginnings the basic forms of architecture and of sculpture are identical; that is to say, in so far as sculpture aspires to monumentality, and in so far as architecture aspires to symbolic meaning and durability, the two arts make common use of the same material, stone, and endow this material with identical plastic values. The perfect demonstration of this unity is found in certain Indian temples carved out of solid rock, and there are many examples of monumental sculpture, from the Pyramids in Egypt to the Victor Emmanuel monument in Rome, that are essentially architectural in effect. But this is perhaps no more significant than the fact that the epic and the lyric make use of the same language; just as these are both aspects of poetics, so architecture and monumental sculpture are both aspects of tectonics.

In so far as the aesthetics of the specific art of architecture are based on the materials of the art – wood, stone, steel – we must seek for a principle in the nature of these materials; and in so far as aesthetics are determined by function or purpose (and we have not yet discussed the validity of such an assumption) we must seek for a principle in the appropriateness of the means to the end. Though both these principles are aspects of truth – truth to materials and truth to functions – there is no obvious connection between them, and we shall therefore be driven either to seek a compromise of some kind, or alternatively to establish a third principle which is commanding enough to resolve these separate principles in some single unifying concept of the art of architecture. I believe that such a concept does exist, but that we have largely lost sight of it in our preoccupation with materialism and functionalism.

Let us start with the obvious proposition that architecture has its origins as an artificial shelter from the elements. Such a shelter must have walls and a roof, but from the beginning variations were possible. The building could be rectangular or round, high or low, wide or narrow; it could be built of wattles or wood, bricks or stones; the interior could be light or dark, cool or warm;

the structure slight or solid. The choice among so many possibilities might be determined by purpose or climate, by the
availability of the raw materials or the defendability of the site.
Primitive architecture can be explained wholly by means of these
material factors, and it has been maintained, by March Phillips
for example, an important writer on the subject to whom I shall
return, that Egyptian art never escaped from these materialistic
factors, that it was 'a perpetuation of the primitive', an art that
'stops short always at the point where intellect should animate
and inspire it'. Where *intellect should* animate and inspire it – there
you have the introduction of a factor that is no longer materialistic, and that is imperative. Architecture, if it is to escape from
the primitive, the childish, the archaic, must be inspired by
considerations that are intellectual, abstract, spiritual – considerations that modify the strict requirements of utility.

I have no desire to question this basic theory: it has been stated
with different emphases but essential agreement by every philosopher of art from Vitruvius to Winckelmann, by Semper,
Ruskin, Lethaby, March Phillips, Worringer and Focillon. It is
the eternally reiterated claim of spirit to inform matter, and art
ceases to exist when that claim is refused. Nevertheless, matter
is recalcitrant and only yields to a spirit capable of an intense
and coherent vision. Aesthetics is the study of the conditions
under which the materials of art are persuaded to accommodate
an informing spirit. It has always been recognized that the Greek
temple is the paradigm for this study, and in spite of all that has
been written about the subject, we cannot do better than return
to that paradigm for an essential insight into the nature of the
problem we are discussing.

Anyone who has visited the Doric temples in Greece, Italy or
Sicily, and has been able to exclude the romantic feelings aroused
by their forlorn isolation, must have had some difficulty in reconciling their architectural prestige with his modern conception
of functionalism. Even as shrines of an arcane cult they must
have been devoid of any internal logic; dark, crowded and
oppressive. As architectural monuments they were designed for

external effect, to be best seen and appreciated from a distance. The basic functional requirement of architecture, shelter from the elements, is therefore not in question. Another peculiarity, often noted for its technical interest, is the fact that they carry over into stone the posts and crossbeams of a primitive wooden structure not particularly suited to the new material. From a functional point of view they seem to be unintelligent imitations of a primitive method of building.

In fact, however, the Greek temples are increasingly sophisticated developments of a basic form, and what began as a utilitarian structure was gradually refined until it became a symbol for spiritual values. These values, when experienced in their coherence and wholeness, are known as beauty, but essentially they are formal quantities and can be expressed mathematically; we call them harmony, balance and symmetry. Greek architecture is an attempt to create a plastic image that, like Greek poetry or Greek music or Greek ceramics, expresses the idea that *proportion* is one of the highest values in human life,[3] and critics like Conrad Fiedler and March Phillips have rightly characterized it as intellectual. Fiedler speaks of a long period of artistic stammering, a striving and struggling for the right expression until finally perfection is attained as a result of an association of the clarity of consciousness with the greatest force of thought. All the material elements of the structure are fused, as it were, into a purified image of harmonious form. He quotes Semper's axiom – Art invents nothing; and then asserts: 'The Greeks invented nothing in their architecture, but developed only that which they received, and with such a clear awareness that they necessarily arrived at a result in which everything directly reminiscent of the demands of needs and wants, of the nature of the material used and of the conditions of construction, had disappeared except for faint echoes.'[4]

March Phillips, in his great but neglected book, *The Works of Man*,[5] gives an even greater emphasis to the essentially intellectual nature of the Greek achievement. The most striking consequences of this intellectual bias and the limitations it imposed

40. The Parthenon. 448-432 BC

41.   *East Portico, The Erechtheum, c.421 BC*

42.   *Temple of Olympian Zeu*
The Olympeum.   Completed AD 131–13

are to be found, he suggests, 'in the Greek love of the definite and in the Greek passion for definition. All that is clear-cut and articulate the Greek mind adores; all that is in the least vague and indeterminate it detests . . . [The Greeks], for the first time, exploited the idea of intellectual definition, and it soon followed that they would admit no thought which would not submit itself to definition.'

There is, however, some equivocation about this process of definition. March Phillips recollects that there are certain spiritual qualities that will not submit to definition – that Nature herself when endued with an infinite significance 'becomes shrouded in a kind of mystery, and the thoughts and feelings she suggests do not admit of articulation and refuse to be exactly defined'. In this manner he raises a question about the cognitive status of art which he does not stop to answer. We are entitled to ask in what sense a Greek temple is a definition of ideas or concepts that a Gothic cathedral is not also a definition of ideas and concepts? Surely it is the ideas that differ, not the process of definition. 'The clear-cut, cameo-like quality of Greek thought' is one concept, somewhat sentimentally expressed; and what Goethe called 'the shapeless and intangible forms of the sublime' is another concept. Greek thought got its cameo-like quality from the long process of refinement I have already referred to; but 'the shapeless and intangible forms of the sublime' were also in their turn subjected to a process of refinement and the result was Gothic architecture. The same will to form was acting upon different spiritual concepts.

For Conrad Fiedler Gothic architecture is a by-road, even an impasse, the pointed arch an evasion of the refining process of the intellect. 'To the impartial and enlightened eye, the entire Gothic style will be a phenomenon which is essentially a side-path leading away from the road which all art must travel, no matter how much it bears witness to various excellent human capabilities. It [Gothic architecture] is entirely isolated for, in the obstinacy of its peculiar purpose, it broke away from that which awaited gradual development. When an artistic need was again

43. Gio Ponti. Pirelli building, Milan. 1958

felt in architectural activity, no points of contact were found in the Gothic style.'[6]

Fiedler was writing in 1878. We would not today so confidently assert that modern architecture had found no points of contact with Gothic architecture. Ponti's Pirelli building in Milan (*Plate 43*), to take only one example, is more Gothic than Greek; and yet it has the intellectual clarity of a precise form; and so, for that matter, has the nave of Cologne cathedral (*Plate 46*), or any other completely realized architectural concept of the Gothic period. It is true that some of the early Gothic cathedrals, such as Durham, derive their power from their embodiment of numinous in-tuitions rather than from any intellectual refinement of their proportions, and Gothic form is often difficult to disinter from its piecemeal construction: the conceptions were too ambitious for immediate achievement, and were sometimes muddled or modi-fied by successive builders. But as Otto von Simson has shown, in his book on *The Gothic Cathedral*,[7] the ideals that inspired the Abbot Suger in the building of Saint-Denis (*Plate 44*), the first full conception of the Gothic cathedral, were precise enough, and through the mediation of St Augustine and Dionysus the Pseudo-Areopagite, were derived from classical sources. Gothic form is a strict application of the Greek ideals of harmony and proportion. It is simply untrue, therefore, to assert, as does Fiedler, that the Gothic style has no points of contact with the Greek tradition; on the contrary, in its most essential features, it is a continuation of this tradition with new modes of construction. The purpose of the new structures was indeed far from the Greek spirit, for the God to be worshipped in them was transcendent and his symbol was the light of Heaven, but the same intellectual passion was directed to the clear realization of these symbolic values in a precise architectural form.

The real distinction between Greek and Gothic architecture is not intellectual: it is not even a distinction of material, for both depend on stone. It is fundamentally a difference of approach to the same material, with the same tools and the same measures. The results are different because the informing spirit is different.

Worringer stated the difference in this way: 'the Greek architect approached his material, stone, with a certain sensuousness and therefore allowed the material to express itself as such. But the Gothic architect approached stone with a desire for purely spiritual expression, that is to say, with structural intentions conceived artistically and independently of stone, and for which stone was only the external and submissive means of realization. An abstract system of contruction is the result, wherein the stone plays a merely practical and not artistic part.'[8] Or more clearly still: 'Greek architecture is applied construction, Gothic architecture is pure construction. The constructive element in the first case is merely the means to a practical end; in the latter case it is an end in itself, for it coincides with artistic intentions of expression.'[9] Gothic architecture, therefore, might be said to be a better illustration of Fiedler's ideal, because we can say more truly of the Gothic cathedral than of the Greek temple that it 'has attained the supreme result in a given field; nothing in the structure is presented to our view except form, and the complete intellectualization of all material elements causes the structure to appear removed from material existence'.[10]

This misconception of Gothic arose in the Age of Enlightenment, when men could no longer believe in a transcendent God and returned to the ideals of Greek humanism. Gothic, because it was an invention of the North, was identified with barbarism, and the fact that its inventors had derived their ideals of proportion from the Greeks was ignored. We might say in explanation that at this time the concept of 'style' began to replace the concept of 'form', and it therefore became possible to condemn the art of a period for subjective reasons.

I do not wish to draw a parallel between form in classicism and style in romanticism, but style is fluid, intangible, indefinite, only to be described by analogies; whereas form is definite, definable, measurable, open to analysis. This does not mean that form is always logical or rational: we live in a period that has learned to appreciate irregular forms. But one can say that form is archetypal or universal, whereas style is individual or regional.

In this sense Baroque architecture, often associated with the Counter-Reformation, is to be regarded as almost wholly a stylistic phenomenon: as a face-lift for an effete classicism. Fiedler's essay on architecture was never completed, but the strictures he made on Gothic architecture should have been reserved for Baroque; here, if anywhere, was an evasion of the higher demands of form, and though the architectural form was not mutilated to solve a practical problem, which is Fiedler's charge against Gothic, it was nevertheless ignored to solve an emotional problem: to make architecture a pictorial (picturesque) rather than a plastic reality. The greatest exponent of the Baroque style in architecture is Bernini (*Plate 49*); it is no paradox that he is also the greatest of the Baroque sculptors. Sculpture, architecture, all plastic means are subordinated to an operatic totality designed for emotional stimulation and not for serene contemplation. His best apologist, Professor Wittkower, has admitted that Bernini's aim was to create 'a supra-real world in which the transitions seem obliterated between real and imaginary space, past and present, phenomenal and actual existence, life and death'; and Wittkower suggests that 'this urge to use all the means of illusion in the theatre as well as in religious imagery, to try and transport the individual into another reality, seems ultimately connected with the polarity between self-reliance and authority, reason and faith, which afflicted western man seriously for the first time in the seventeenth century: it was the road of escape for those who began to doubt.'[11] But it was not the road which, according to Fiedler, 'all art must travel, no matter how much it bears witness to various excellent human capabilities'.

Let us return to our first principle, that architecture is the art of enclosing space. There are two basic elements: space, and the material used to enclose it. For a work of art to emerge from the process it is essential that these two basic elements should produce a unified effect. It is not enough that the space alone should be effective; and it is not enough that the envelope enclosing the space should be effective. The art is in the effective synthesis of these two elements.

44. Abbey of St-Denis. Suger's Ambulatory. 12th century

45. *The Nave, Durham Cathedral. 12th century*

46. *The Nave, St Peter's Cathedral, Cologne. 13th century*

47. *Sant' Apollinare in Classe, Ravenna.*   AD 535-549

48. *Sancta Sophia, Istanbul.*   AD 532-537

If this is accepted as an elementary axiom, then we must conclude that classical architecture never reached artistic perfection – that it remained a lapidary art to be judged by its external proportions. In other words, it was never decisively emancipated from the sculptural complex in which it originated. It is not until we come to the Romanesque period that a sensibility for space begins to swell the interior space to some expressive purpose. The device that enabled the architect to produce this effect was, of course, the vault, and vault construction, a substructure in antiquity, was, in the striking words used by Fiedler, to rise from a subterranean existence to the light of day and develop anew. What had been a structural convenience was seized on for its expressive qualities, and its articulation is the key to the process by means of which architectural unity was to be achieved. But the development would not have taken place unless an essentially sculptural feeling for mass had been replaced by an essentially architectural feeling for space – the idea, which the vault made possible, that a building could rise from the ground rather than rest on it. This, as I think Fiedler was the first to appreciate, was the simple point of departure for a new architectonic development which gave to the art of architecture its unique aesthetic qualities.

It is not necessary for me to re-trace the subsequent development of the spatial concept in Romanesque and Byzantine architecture, but it should be noted that in the excitement of this new discovery, the architects of the Christian basilica (*Plate 47*) tended to concentrate on the interior and to neglect the exterior, which often gives the impression of a garment turned outside in. Unity remains an ideal, only rarely to be achieved, and no country and no religion has an exclusive claim to it. Nevertheless, the great centrally planned Byzantine churches remain the prototypes of architectural unity, for they alone of all the buildings of the past are organically articulated. If we are aware of this effect, it is probably because, as Professor Michelis has pointed out, the unity of the enclosed space is stressed by the central dome. 'In diverging towards the perimeter from the dome, the central space makes a centrifugal movement: it is not placed there by the addition of independent spaces around the centre, as in Roman buildings like the Parthenon or the Baths of Caracalla: it is a branching off, an organic development. Height, moreover, is self-emphasized in a natural ascent towards the light, along with the gradual rise of the vaults supporting the dome. Thus, as reproductions of the Universe, the churches aimed to convey the sublime idea of the Omnipotent Spirit through infinite, but unified, space.'[12] Sancta Sophia (*Plate 48*) is the supreme example of such architectural sublimity, and it should always be remembered that it was the work of Greek architects in a Greek city.[13]

It must be emphasized that sublimity, in connection with Sancta Sophia or any other great building, is an effect of unity, and that such unity is achieved by logic, by the intellect in the service of an idea. This does not mean that art is rationalistic, but rather that reason is in the service of art, to attain that clarity of consciousness, that plastic definition, by means of which the work of art, as icon, can best secure its emotive or symbolic effect. One might say, with Wordsworth, that the 'pure motions of the sense . . . seem, in their simplicity, to own an intellectual charm'.

I shall now turn, somewhat abruptly, to a consideration of modern architecture, for having established this principle of spatio-plastic unity as the distinctive characteristic of architecture as an art, we can now ask to what extent the architecture of our own time has attained it.

Modern architecture, like Gothic architecture, is an exploitation of new technical devices; to these it adds an exploitation of new materials like concrete and steel. Its most essential characteristic is a principle of construction that no longer relies on a rigid shell – the bearing walls have been eliminated and have been replaced by an internal skeleton of steel on which the walls hang like curtains. It is 'a skin and bone construction'.[14]

A second and perhaps equally important characteristic is due to the fact that the building materials are for the most part machine-made and pre-fabricated. The materials of all previous styles of architecture – wood, stone, brick – were shaped by hand and could be made to the requirements of the individual architect. Modern building materials are standardized and the economics of modern architecture are such that it is impossible to work with materials that are not machine-made and standardized. This is not necessarily an impossible limitation on the aesthetic potentialities of the art – the composer of music has a limited scale of notes of a pre-determined value.

The modern architect has made a virtue of these necessities; that is to say, he has accepted a discipline of form determined by the nature of the materials available to him and is satisfied if by these means he can create a building that serves its purpose. Rational order, clarity, economy – such are the values he strives to embody in his building. He consciously eschews 'all esthetic speculation, all doctrine, all formalism'. These again are the words of one of the greatest of modern architects, Mies van der Rohe (*Plate 51*), who further has said: 'Form is not the aim of our work, but only the result. Form, by itself, does not exist. Form as an aim is formalism; and that we reject.'[15]

Let me, for the sake of contrast, recall Fiedler's words: 'In architecture, as in every intellectual activity, there is a progress from the formless to the formed . . . Forms which owe their existence to needs and wants, or to technical ability, are, so to say, moulded from outside according to certain independently formulated requirements . . . [The] artistic process of creation in architecture is characterized by an alteration of form whereby materials and constructions continue to recede, while the form which belongs to the intellect, continues to develop towards an increasingly independent existence.'[16]

A complete contradiction! We must do our best to resolve it, for Fiedler and Mies cannot both be right. They are on opposite sides of this question, which is the question of formalism in architecture. (Incidentally we may note that the discussion of this problem is not confined to architecture: it rages in all the arts.)

The aphorisms I have quoted from Mies date from 1923. Unlike most of our leading architects, Mies does not often resort to writing and propaganda, but there is a later and more considered statement of his aims which he made in an inaugural address as Director of Architecture at the Armour Institute of Architecture in 1938. In this address he distinguishes between 'practical aims', which he says are 'bound to the specific structure of our epoch' and 'values' which are 'rooted in the spiritual nature of man'. He then admits that though architecture 'in its simplest form' is rooted in entirely functional considerations, 'it can reach up through all degrees of value to the highest sphere of spiritual existence, into the realm of pure art'.

He then remarks what feeling for material and what power of expression the great buildings of the past possessed, and how the power of expression comes from the discipline of the materials used. He says that all this is no less true of steel and concrete: 'everything depends on how we use a material, not on the material itself'. How it is used will depend on the functions of the building, and on certain psychological or spiritual factors, for in the end we are dependent on 'the spirit of our time'. Three different principles of order are available to the architect: the *mechanistic* which overemphaizes the materialistic and functionalistic factors in life; the *idealistic* which overemphasizes the ideal and the formal; and the *organic* which alone achieves the successful relationship of the parts to each other and to the whole. Mies takes his stand on this organic principle of order and here he sets himself alongside a modern architect who superficially would seem to be very different in practice and style, Frank Lloyd Wright – 'a master-builder', as Mies has called him, 'drawing upon the veritable fountainhead of architecture; who with true originality lifted his creations into the light. Here again, at long last, genuine organic architecture flowered.'[17]

I do not know whether Frank Lloyd Wright (*Plate 52*) was the first architect to use this word 'organic' to describe his principles. He tells us in his *Autobiography* that when he married at the age of twenty-one, Sullivan, to whom he was apprenticed, allowed him to build a house for himself, and that he carved in the oak slab above the fireplace in the living room, 'Truth is Life'. A

50. *Walter Gropius
and Louis McMillen.
Entrance Arch,
University of Baghdad.
Under construction.*

51. *Mies van der Rohe.
Seagram Building,
New York. 1958.*

52. *Frank Lloyd Wright. Kaufmann House, 'Falling Water'. 1936*

challenge to sentimentality, he then thought; and soon after it occurred to him that 'Life is Truth'. That was in the year 1888, and that is perhaps the moment when the idea of an organic architecture was born. It was an idea that grew with his work, and which was still growing when he died seventy years later.

Frank Lloyd Wright often defined what he meant by organic architecture, and though the best definition is to be found in his buildings, I like to recall one that I was privileged to hear when he lectured in London in 1939. Perhaps the most important statement he made on that occasion was that organic achitecture implies an organic society. He also said that 'the word "organic" does not, cannot apply to so-called classic architecture in any form whatsoever, and it does not apply to any of the "period" buildings, even the "Georgian" in which we live today. The term does not apply to anything else we happen to have. It would apply however to the old Japanese buildings; Japanese domestic architecture was truly organic architecture. It would apply to certain other periods in the architecture of the world. Egyptian architecture was in a sense organic architecture, an expression of the feeling for human form. The Gothic cathedrals in the Middle Ages had much in them that was organic in character, and they became influential and beautiful, in so far as that quality lived in them which was *organic*, as did all other architectures possessing it. Greek architecture knew it – not at all! It was the supreme search for the elegant solution.'[18]

This is a definition by enumeration, but it serves to make clear that Frank Lloyd Wright, equally with Mies van der Rohe, would reject the intellectual ideal of form represented by Greek architecture as interpreted by Fiedler, and represented by Gothic architecture as interpreted by von Simson. But before we slip into the easy solution of accepting this organic principle as obviously the right one, let us realize a little more clearly its implications. We have to ask what Wright meant by an organic society, and we know, from his many statements of the ideal, that it was something decidedly inconsistent with 'the spirit of our time' upon which, according to Mies van der Rohe, the architect is and should be dependent. Mies described Wright as 'a giant tree in a wide landscape', a metaphor which well suits his isolation. He was against all the cherished ideals of our civilization – he was against skyscrapers, he was against cities, he was against civilization itself. He was for decentralization, distribution, individualism. 'Life', he wrote at the end of his *Autobiography*, 'always rides in strength to victory, not through internationalism or through any other "isms", but only through the direct responsibility of the individual. It bears a royal characteristic called Initiative. Where individual initiative is active, strong and operative, there you may see the mainspring of life in abundance, operating.' And his conclusion might well be ours – 'Organic Democratic FORM: TRUTH ever fresh has not yet come to our Civilization.'[19]

A sober conclusion: and yet I linger over the word FORM. What does it imply, in an organic or any other context? There I think Fiedler, and the whole classic sense of order, perhaps mediated to Fiedler through Goethe, still has some relevance. There is, in the immediate world of our sensations, no such thing as Form, but only a profusion of forms. And surely Fiedler was right in insisting that there must be a process of refinement in which the genuine is separated from the false, or shall we rather say, the vital from the dead. 'The motley wealth of forms must disappear, and all creating power must express itself in such a manner that, in the ever near and ever more perfect, sought-for expression, the given great thoughts of form expand to ever higher clarity and perfection. Only thus is an architectural style, in the true sense of the word, created.'[20] Clarity and perfection are words used by Mies van der Rohe, though not conspicuously by Wright. What I am searching for, in conclusion, is some formula that would combine individual initiative with universal values, and that combination would give us a truly organic form. Form, which we discover in nature by analysis, is obstinately mathematical in its manifestations – which is to say that its creation in art requires thought and deliberation. But this is not to say that form can be reduced to a formula. In every work of art it must be recreated, but that too is true of every work of nature. Art differs from nature, not in its organic form, but in its human origins: in the fact that it is not God or a machine that makes a work of art, but an individual with his instincts and his intuitions, with his sensibility and his mind, searching restlessly for the perfection that is neither in mind nor in nature, but in the unknown. I do not mean this in any other-worldly sense: only in the sense that the form of the flower is unknown to the seed.

A very perceptive American critic, Roger Shattuck, has recently suggested that what distinguishes the modern movement in the arts is the rejection of the principle of unity. The modern sensibility, at the turn of the century, 'began to proceed not so much by untrammelled expansion of the unities as by a violent dislocation of them in order to test the possibility of a new coherence . . . a work of art began to coordinate as equally present a variety of time and places and states of consciousness. The process, because it seeks to hold these elements in a meaning-ful relationship, relinquishes both classic unity and also the quality of self-forgetfulness which characterizes romanticism.' *'Juxta-position* is the key-word of this new sensibility; setting one thing beside the other without connective. The twentieth century has addressed itself to arts of juxtaposition as opposed to earlier arts of *transition*.'[21]

If style is thus related to unity, Mies would seem to be a classic artist, Wright a romantic one. Is there then an architecture that would correspond to the art of 'juxtaposition' – to the cubism of Gris, the poetry of Apollinaire, to serial music and the fiction of Proust? Mr Shattuck believes that there is, and that one of its most successful manifestations has been 'functional' architecture which 'allows all parts to show in a building as if they constituted its subconscious'. The subconscious of a building is a difficult concept, and it would hardly have appealed to a formalist like Fiedler. But in the sense that 'any form of decoration, transition, or arbitrarily imposed symmetry' is a mask designed to hide the discontinuous parts or functions of a building, in that sense the metaphor serves to describe the 'brutalism' of which many of our younger architects have made an aesthetic virtue. Architecture, too, can become an arrangement of fragments of experience, 'a complex art, perishable perhaps, of self-awareness'. Its unity must now be conceived as an equilibrium of forces, a state of arrested movement, of tension – not as the expression of intellectual clarity.

It would be against all historical precedent if modern architecture were not to show some sympathy with the arts contemporary with it, and there is no doubt that the characteristic arts of our time show just these features of juxtaposition, of disparate but corresponding states of consciousness, attributed to them by Mr Shattuck. But Mr Shattuck is ready to admit that works of art must nevertheless aspire to 'the simple stability of monuments', and that an equilibrium of forces does not achieve artistic validity until that equilibrium becomes a condition of absolute stillness. In this I agree: modern architecture may be as nakedly functional and fragmented as anyone chooses, but in so far as it aspires to be an art it must be an organization of form that we can contemplate with serenity because it is emancipated from time, the antithesis of art. Art, in its highest manifestations, has always been a true measure that reconciles all material elements and all spiritual forces in harmonious unity. The material elements change from age to age, and so do the spiritual forces: the principle of formal unity remains constant and imperative.

VI

The Poet and his Muse

THE ORIGINS OF FORM IN POETRY

Foole saide my Muse to mee, looke in thy heart and write.
SIDNEY

I

My intention is to show how the myth or image of the Muse in art personifies certain stratagems of the creative imagination that enable the artist to endow this form of his work with universal significance. For my evidence I shall rely on the poets rather than other types of artists, but I believe that the principles to be established hold good for all the arts.

Let me first dispose of one ambiguity: we speak of 'creation' or 'origination' knowing full well that there is nothing new under the sun, and that no artist, within the limits of human comprehension, has the divine faculty of bringing a new order out of chaos. I have dealt with such ambiguities in the first essay in this volume, and have elsewhere shown in what sense we may say that the poet 'bodies forth the forms of things unknown'.[1] Long usage, however, has justified the use of these metaphorical words for the process by means of which the poet or painter or composer of music combines into a new and newly significant order the images which he takes from his memory: the Muses, from the beginning, were the daughters of Mnemosyne, or memory.

Eranos Jahrbuch, XXI, 1962. Zurich (Rhein Verlag), 1963.

One further preliminary disclaimer. I shall not speculate on the mythology of the Muses, fascinating as this is. There were orginally the Nine Muses of classical mythology, representing, with a significance that should not be lost to our divided culture, the sciences as well as the arts. The concepts of a single Muse, always feminine, was already present in classical times, but her sphere, when not specified, was not necessarily one of the arts. With the decline of classical mythology the Nine Muses tended to merge into one Muse, though a Muse accessible to more than one kind of artist. Orpheus, the son of Calliope, and perhaps of Apollo, was to assume a special significance as the personification of the magical power of lyrical poetry, and is often invoked instead of the Muse.

The classical Muses were tutelary – that is to say, goddesses responsible for the general well-being of their respective spheres of activity rather than for the inspiration of individual artists. It is perhaps not too fanciful to suggest that the guardian angel of Christian iconography is a transformation of the classical Muse endowed with a similar tutelary function. In the greatest of Christian poems Beatrice appears at the beginning as the poet's Muse:

> Io era tra color, che son sospesi,
> e donna mi chiamò beata e bella
> tal che di comandare io la richiesi

'I was amongst them who are in suspense; and a Lady, so far and blessed that I prayed her to command, called me.' It is Beatrice who commands Virgil to guide Dante on his way. Inspired by Beatrice, Virgil becomes *duca, signore, e maestro* – guide, lord and master of the poet.[2]

But this is not exactly our modern conception of the poet's Muse, nor indeed was it necessarily the classical tradition. Already in Plato we find two further implications, the first having to do with the fact that the Muses were the daughters of Mnemosyne, or memory; the second with the supposition that to invoke their aid was to risk losing one's reason.

In the dialogue named after Theaetetus, Socrates asks the young mathematician to imagine, for the sake of argument, that our minds contain a block of wax, which in this or that individual may be larger or smaller, and composed of wax that is comparatively pure or muddy, harder in some, softer in others, and sometimes of just the right consistency. This block of wax is the gift of Memory, the mother of the Muses, and the argument proceeds to show that knowledge of reality will depend on the distinctness of the images recorded by the wax – it is reliable only when the wax is of exactly the right consistency. The Muses in this fanciful metaphor thus act as intermediaries between the Self and Reality: the Self cannot have any true knowledge of Reality without their aid.

In the *Ion* Plato uses another metaphor, that of the magnet or load-stone. The Muse holds a series of rings, and through these rings her magic passes like an invisible force to the poets who cling to them. 'One poet is suspended from one Muse, another from another; we call it being "possessed", but the fact is much the same, since he is *held*. And from these primary rings [the poets], others are in turn suspended, some attached to this one, some to that, and are filled with inspiration, some by Orpheus, others by Musaeus. But the majority are possessed and held by Homer . . .'[3]

This is really a very deterministic theory of memory and inspiration. There is a divine source of wisdom – this is taken as self-evident; this wisdom is transmitted in a causal sequence from Jupiter and Mnemosyne to their children, the Muses, and from the Muses in turn to their children. Though originally reputed to be virgins who successfully defended their chastity, most of the Muses gradually fell from this state of grace. Calliope had three sons, Hymenaeus, Ialemus and Orpheus; Melpomene lay with the river-god Achelous and begat the Sirens; Euterpe had Rhesus for a son and Clio Hyacinthus. Thalia gave birth to the Corybantes; again Apollo was the father and he competes with Amphimarus, a musician, for the fathership of Linus, the son of Urania. Thamyris was the son of Erato, and Triptolemus of

Polyhymnia. In such manner the propagation of the arts was secured.

From one of these children of the Muses the divine spark was transmitted to Homer and from Homer, the father of all poets, to the lesser epic and lyric poets. When the magnetic force reaches the lesser poets, they are 'seized with the Bacchic transport, and are possessed'. And this is where Socrates's famous description of the poet occurs, as one who 'is a light and winged thing, and holy, and never able to compose until he has become inspired, *and is beside himself, and reason is no longer in him*'.[4]

I emphasize these last words, because they describe very clearly the dichotomy in the inspired poet, the sense of two beings, *Führer* and *Geführter*, leader and led. To make his meaning clear, Socrates gives the example of Tynnichus of Chalcis. 'He never composed a single poem worth recalling, save the song of praise which everyone repeats, well-nigh the finest of all lyrical poems, and absolutely what he called it, an "Invention of the Muses". By this example above all, it seems to me, the god would show us, lest we doubt, that these lovely poems are not of man or human workmanship, but are divine and from the gods, and that the poets are nothing but interpreters of the gods, each one possessed by the divinity to whom he is in bondage.'[5]

This, then, is the classical conception of the Muse; a deity who for the occasion deprives a human being of his senses and uses him as the witless mouthpiece of divine utterance. It is not a conception that is very flattering to the poet as an intelligent human being, and this explains why it was possible for Plato to have a low opinion of the poet while retaining the highest respect for poetry. It is, of course, a conception that has persisted wherever the classical tradition has survived, and it is still possible to regard the best poets and artists of all kinds as childlike or naïve people who inexplicably give birth to works of genius. In a certain sense this has become the popular and even vulgar conception of the poet; any other conception will seem relatively sophisticated.

The Renaissance introduced a typical modification of the classical conception of the Muse. I shall take as my example

Milton, not only because he is a great poet of my own tongue, but also because he was a man of great learning and in this respect is representative of the European Renaissance in general.

Paradise Lost opens with an invocation to a 'Heav'nly Muse':

> Of Mans First Disobedience, and the Fruit
> Of that Forbidden Tree . . .
> Sing Heav'nly Muse, that on the secret top
> Of *Oreb*, or of *Sinai*, didst inspire
> That Shepherd, who first taught the chosen Seed,
> In the Beginning how the Heav'ns and Earth
> Rose out of *Chaos:* or if *Sion* Hill
> Delight thee more, and *Siloa's* Brook that flow'd
> Fast by the Oracle of God; I thence
> Invoke thy aid to my adventurous Song,
> That with no middle flight intends to soar
> Above th'*Aonion* Mount, while it pursues
> Things unattempted yet in Prose or Rhime
> And chiefly Thou O Spirit, that dost prefer
> Before all Temples th'upright heart and pure,
> Instruct me, for Thou know'st; Thou from the first
> Wast present, and with mighty wings outspread
> Dove-like satst brooding on the vast Abyss
> And mad'st it pregnant: What in me is dark
> Illumin, what is low raise and support;
> That to the highth of this great Argument
> I may assert Eternal Providence,
> And justifie the wayes of God to men.

This invocation is addressed to an all-seeing power, an all-pervading spirit that will aid the poet in his adventurous song. By comparison with the classical Muses, who also were heavenly but feminine and fallible, Milton's Muse is dove-like, brooding, as sexless as the angels. Dante's Beatrice, though an angel, disclosed when we first encounter her sitting in Heaven with 'the ancient Rachel', has human traits, comparable to those of the Beatrice Dante had known on earth. Milton tells us that his Muse is the same that had inspired the shepherd Moses on Mount

Horeb, and later as a leader of his people on Mount Sinai. But
Milton gives examples of other places where biblical inspiration
had taken place – Sion Hill and Siloa's brook, and even mentions
in passing, as an inferior station, the classical source of inspiration,
the Aeonian mount, or Mount Helicon. Classical inspiration, and
even biblical inspiration, was always associated with high places,
with mountains, a tradition as old as Assyria and Babylon, whose
Ziggurats were artificial mountains built to bring men nearer to
the heavenly source of inspiration. But then, in conclusion, Milton
introduces the individualistic, subjective possibility – the possibility that the Spirit might prefer the pure and upright heart
before any geographical site. Inspiration does not depend on
temples or holy places: it can be a direct visitation to the mind of
man. But it remains a distinct and tutelary force and is not yet to
be identified with human consciousness.

The opening invocation is not, however, the only reference to
the Muse in *Paradise Lost*. Book VII opens with an equally eloquent
and even longer invocation, and this time the Heavenly Muse is
identified with one of the classical Muses, Urania, the Muse of
astronomy. Milton is somewhat ambiguous in this second appeal
for inspiration. He wants to make use of the classical conception
of inspiration, but in order to make clear that his inspiration is
divine and not secular, he chooses Urania instead of Calliope, and
even 'the meaning, not the name'. But let us look a little more
closely at this passage in *Paradise Lost*:

> Descend from Heav'n *Urania*, by that name
> If rightly thou art call'd whose Voice divine
> Following, above th'*Olympian* Hill I soare
> Above the flight of *Pegasean* wing.
> The meaning, not the Name I call: for thou
> Nor of the Muses nine, nor on the top
> Of old *Olympus* dwell'st, but Heav'nlie borne,
> Before the Hills appeerd, or Fountain flow'd,
> Thou with Eternal wisdom didst converse,
> Wisdom thy Sister, and with her didst play
> In presence of th'Almightie Father, pleas'd

With thy Celestial Song. Up led by thee
Into the Heav'n of Heav'ns I have presum'd,
An Earthlie Guest, and drawn Empyreal Aire,
Thy tempring; with like safetie guided down
Return me to my Native Element:
. . .
Standing on Earth, not rapt above the Pole,
More safe I Sing with mortal voice, unchang'd
To hoarce or mute, though fall'n on evil dayes,
On evil dayes though fall'n, and evil tongues;
In darkness, and with dangers compast round,
And solitude; yet not alone, while thou
Visit'st my slumbers Nightly, or when Morn
Purples the East: still govern thou my Song,
Urania, and fit audience find, though few.

It will be seen that we have returned to the upright heart and pure,
but this time the Muse is specific and feminine, Urania, the Muse
of the heavenly spheres, the sister of Wisdom. Then, to make
quite clear that he has nothing to do with Calliope, the rather
earthy Muse of heroic poetry, the mistress of Apollo and mother
of Orpheus, Milton bids Urania

. . . drive farr off the barbarous dissonance
Of *Bacchus* and his Revellers, the Race
Of that wilde Rout that tore the *Thracian* Bard
In *Rhodope*, where Woods and Rocks had Eares
To rapture, till the savage clamor dround
Both Harp and Voice; nor could the Muse defend
Her Son. So fail not thou, who thee implores:
For thou art Heave'nlie, shee an empty dreame.

I do not wish to discuss the various sources of inspiration indicated
by the poets, but rather the process common to them all. Milton
wishes to distinguish (and to claim for himself) divine inspiration
as opposed to merely poetic or lyrical inspiration. But he still
maintains the original classical conception of an external source
of inspiration, a feminine archetype endowed with wisdom,

foresight and omniscience, who, when appealed to, guides the poet in his epic narration, revives his memory, brings illumination and ensures the truth of his great argument, a 'celestial patroness', who comes 'unimplored'

> And dictates to him slumbering, or inspires
> Easy his unpremeditated verse.

I will leave Milton as representative of the relation of the Renaissance poet to his Muse and turn now to the Romantic poets, in whom we find a gradual modification of the conception. For the sake of brevity I shall confine myself to three poets, Blake, Shelley and Wordsworth, and will then pass on to what might be called the jilting of the Muse by later poets such as Edgar Allan Poe and Paul Valéry. I think we shall then have enough material to substantiate an hypothesis in the second part of this lecture.

Blake is not a complicated case – he believed quite simply that in the act of writing poetry he was being dictated to by heavenly spirits, sometimes anonymous, sometimes recognizable as historical characters. There is not one 'celestial patroness', but many 'angels' or 'authors in Eternity'. 'I have written this Poem from immediate Dictation', he wrote to this friend Thomas Butts (25 April 1803), 'twelve or sometimes twenty lines at a time, without Premeditation & even against my Will; the Time it has taken in writing was thus render'd Non Existent, & an immense Poem Exists which seems to be the Labour of a long Life, all produced without Labour or Study.'[6]

The only point illustrated by Blake that is relevant to my purpose is the dual nature of this process of dictation. The poet is not possessed: he is a detached and passive instrument of a divine purpose. As in Milton's conception of the poet, he is not creative but reproductive, and what he reproduces is a vision, in which not only the images but also the expressive words are 'given'.

Such words are given to him by miscellaneous representatives of the 'Worlds of Eternity'. The Daughters of Memory (the Muses) become the Daughters of Inspiration. The poem Blake called *Milton* opens with an invocation to these Daughters:

Daughters of Beulah! Muses who inspire the Poet's Song,
Record the journey of immortal Milton thro' yon Realms
Of terror and mild moony lustre in soft sexual delusions
Of varied beauty, to delight the wanderer and repose
His burning thirst & freezing hunger! Come into my hand,
By your mild power descending down the Nerves of my right arm
From out the portals of my Brain, where by your ministry
The Eternal Great Humanity Divine planted his Paradise
And in it caus'd the Spectres of the Dead to take sweet forms
In likeness of himself . . .

The Muse in Blake becomes prophetic, which was also Plato's
sense of the Muse's function. The only difference is that what
Blake would call 'vision' Plato called 'madness' – the deity, he
says, has bereft the lyric poets of their senses, 'and uses them as
ministers, along with soothsayers & godly seers . . . in order that
we listeners may know that it is not they who utter these precious
revelations while their mind is not within them, but that it is the
god himself who speaks, and through them becomes articulate to
us'.[7] Blake expressed contempt for 'the Stolen and Perverted
Writings of Homer & Ovid, of Plato & Cicero', because, he said,
their writings were 'set up by artifice against the Sublime of the
Bible',[8] but his own writings make use of the same artifices.

Shelley was, of course, much more directly and much more
consciously indebted to Plato than Blake, but Shelley was a child
of the Enlightenment, the first poet consciously of a scientific
age, and though he does not surrender the special nature of the
poetical faculty, he seeks (but does not find) an explanation of
inspiration within the human mind, being in this respect as much
a psychologist as Coleridge.[9] Poetry, he says, 'ascends to bring
light and fire from those eternal regions where the owl-winged
faculty of calculation dare not ever soar. Poetry is not like
reasoning, a power to be exerted according to the determination
of the will.' He then gives us the beautiful metaphor of the mind
in creation being 'as a fading coal, which some invisible influence,
like an inconstant wind, awakens to transitory brightness'; and
this power, he observes, *arises from within*, and 'the conscious

portions of our nature are unprophetic either of its approach or its departure'. Shelley ends by observing that the same process takes place in the plastic and pictorial arts, but 'the very mind which directs the hands in formation, is incapable of accounting to itself, for the origin, the gradations, or the media of the process'.[10]

In some of his poems Shelley pays conventional tribute to the Muse – Urania herself is invoked in *Adonais*. But his own conception of the source of inspiration is found in the 'Hymn to Intellectual Beauty'. There we have the abstract notion of an 'unseen Power' 'visiting This various world with an inconstant Wing As summer winds that creep from flower to flower', and this power is invoked as:

> Spirit of *Beauty*, that dost consecrate
>> With thine own hues all thou dost shine upon
>> Of human thought or form . . .

The names of 'Demon, Ghost and Heaven' are dismissed as:

> Frail spells – whose uttered charm will not avail to sever,
>> From all we hear and all we see,
>> Doubt, chance, and mutability.

And then the Spirit of Beauty is again invoked as alone capable of giving 'grace and truth to life's unquiet dream'. The poet relates how 'while yet a boy' he had vowed to dedicate his powers to this 'awful *Loveliness*', and invites this power,

> which like the truth
> Of nature on my passive youth
> Descended,

to supply its calm to his 'onward life', and bind him 'to fear himself, and love all human kind'.

The Muse is thus depersonified and becomes an abstract force, still external in origin, but consecrating with its own hues all that of human thought and form it may shine upon. If pressed for a rational explanation of the nature of this external force, Shelley would have taken refuge in nescience. Poetry, he suggests, is 'created by the imperial faculty whose throne is curtained within the invisible nature of man'. At this point we already look forward to a psychology of the unconscious.

I have mentioned Shelley before Wordsworth because in the evolution of the theory of poetry, Wordsworth was, in spite of being the older man, less bound to the classical concepts, more scientifically or analytically aware of the workings of the unconscious – he uses the very word:

> *Unconscious* intercourse with beauty
> Old as creation, drinking in a pure
> Organic pleasure from the silver wreaths
> Of curling mist.

He refers (in the 'Preface to the Lyrical Ballads') to the poet's ability to conjure up in himself 'passions which are indeed far from being the same as those produced by real events, yet do more nearly resemble the passions produced by real events than anything which, from the motion of their own minds merely, other men are accustomed to feel in themselves: – whence, and from practice, he has acquired a greater readiness and power in expressing what he thinks and feels, and especially those thoughts and feelings which, by his own choice, or *from the structure of his own mind*, arise in him without immediate external excitement'. Wordsworth, more than any other English poet, conceived inspiration as an external force in Nature, a *mana:*

> the earth
> And common face of Nature *spake* to me
> Rememberable things . . .

It is Nature that by 'extrinsic passion' first

> Peopled the mind with forms sublime or fair
> And made me love them.

In his autobiographical poem, *The Prelude*, there are many passages in which he addresses, or invokes, a power external to himself, 'Beings of the hills', or, more abstractly, 'Wisdom and Spirit of the Universe' –

> Thou soul that art the eternity of thought
> Thou givest to forms and images a breath
> And everlasting motion . . .

I have suggested elsewhere that Wordsworth's philosophy has many points of resemblance to Oriental philosophy, more particularly to Taoism, where again one finds the concept of an external force in nature, which the Chinese call *Ch'i*, which is not only the vital force in all art, but in a specific sense a formative agency, endowing the artist's work with rhythm and harmony.

Edgar Allan Poe I mention only because his ideas, which are derived in the main from Shelley, passed into French poetics through Baudelaire and are finally a *point de repère* for the reaction represented by Paul Valéry. There is nothing very original in the theory embodied in the three essays on poetry which Poe wrote: they have had such an effect on the theory of poetry because they were the first attempts to present from the point of view of the poet what Poe called a philosophy of composition, or a rationale of verse. They are the prototypes of the analytical criticism of poetry that has been so popular in our own time. But to explain inspiration we find only such vague generalities as 'a sense of the Beautiful', 'an immortal instinct deep within the spirit of man', a 'struggle to apprehend the supernal Loveliness'. He introduces, as 'sole arbiter' in the choice of words, the dreary concept of Taste, and excludes the Intellect or the Conscience. The poetic principle is finally defined, 'strictly and simply', as 'the Human Aspiration for Supernal Beauty', and 'the manifestation of the Principle is always found in *an elevating excitement of the soul*'.

Wordsworth's 'Wisdom and Spirit of the Universe', like Shelley's 'imperial faculty curtained within the invisible nature of man', is an expression of the growing awareness among the Romantic poets of the unconscious as a source of inspiration, independent of the intellectual faculties of man. All the poets and critics of the early nineteenth century begin to make this distinction – Coleridge and Carlyle in England, Goethe and Schelling in Germany, Poe and Emerson in America, de Musset and Lamartine in France – all are searching towards what Carlyle called the distinction between artificial and natural poetry. 'The artificial', wrote Carlyle, 'is the conscious, mechanical; the natural is the unconscious, dynamical.'. . . 'Unconsciousness is the sign of creation; consciousness at best that of manufacture.'[11]

It was from such poets and essayists that Freud himself derived his concept of the unconscious. He relates that when he was fourteen years old he had been given the collected works of a German writer called Ludwig Börne, and there he had read an essay, written in 1823, with the arresting title 'The Art of Becoming an Original Writer in Three Days'. Freud was never to forget this essay, which recommended a method of free association, and Dr Ernest Jones, Freud's biographer, suggests that Börne's 'startling proposal' had sunk into his mind to become the foundation of his psycho-analytical method.[12] One quotation from Börne will show his relevance to our present enquiry:

'To be creative one must be alone, away from people, from books, and as far as possible, from memories. The true act of self-education lies in making oneself unwitting.'

Much more evidence of this kind could be quoted,[13] to emphasize the gradual evolution of the concept of the Unconscious during the past century and a half, but it is now common knowledge and the point I wish to emphasize is that in the process the Unconscious silently usurped the place formerly occupied in the poetic process by the Muses. But that event has merely complicated the process for us. The Muses were convenient and well-defined archetypes. They had names, they were distinct personalities. The poet or any other kind of artist could appeal to them as to a mother or a mistress, and establish an objective relationship. But the Unconscious – how is that amorphous entity to help the poet? It has been shown to be a seething cauldron, full of ugly shapes, a realm of warring shadows, indefinite in extent, fathomless in depth. It is true that it has some connection with memory, the mother of the Muses, and it will, under the right conditions, release some of the innumerable images that are stored there, 'curtained within'. But all that intangible riot would not constitute poetry, or even the basic material of poetry. The Muses were cast for a role of intercession with their mother: memory had nine spheres, carefully defined, and within each sphere the appropriate Muse had established an order – had reduced the confusion of memory to rhythm and harmony. It was for these formal gifts that the ancient poets had recourse to the Muse, and though it is always assumed that the poet had to be in a condition of transport or possession to make contact with the Muse, what he then received was a gift of art, or order, and not of babbling confusion. The classical Muse, therefore, is a *deus ex machina*, the governess of an unruly child, and in no sense to be identified with the unconscious as such.

Before we enquire whether the prevailing theories of the unconscious suggest any mental process that would correspond to the function of the Muse in poetic creation, I should like to bring the theories of Paul Valéry into evidence. Valéry, perhaps the most self-analytical of the great poets of our own time, seems to have been largely indifferent to the claims of psycho-analysis. His introspection was a rigorous discipline that never deviated from the matter in hand – the nature of the poetic process in his own experience. In an early essay (1889) Valéry paid tribute to Poe's 'curious little work *The Philosophy of Composition*'. Himself a mathematician and philosopher, he calls Poe 'mathematician, philosopher and great writer', and of Poe's essay on 'the mechanics of composition' he says:

'None of his works contains more acute analysis or a more strictly logical development of the principles discovered by observation. It is an entirely *a posteriori* technique, based on the psychology of the *listener*, on the knowledge of the different notes that must be sounded in another's soul. Poe's penetrating induction insinuates itself into the reader's intimate reflections,

anticipates and uses them. Well knowing the great part played
in our mental life by habit and automatism, he postulates methods
that since the ancients had been relegated to the inferior genres.
He revives repetition of the same words, which, it seems, was
an Egyptian practice. He predicts with certainty the over-
whelming effect of a bleak refrain, or of frequent alliterations... '[14]

On this essay Valéry was to base what he called a totally new and
modern conception of the poet.

'He is no longer the dishevelled madman who writes a whole
poem in the course of one feverish night; he is a cool scientist,
almost an algebraist, in the service of a subtle dreamer. . . . He
will take care not to hurl on to paper everything whispered to
him in fortunate moments by the Muse of Free Association. On
the contrary, everything he has imagined, felt, dreamed, and
planned will be passed through a sieve, weighed, filtered, subjected
to *form*, and condensed as much as possible so as to gain in power
what it loses in length: a sonnet, for example, will be a true
quintessence, a concentrated and distilled juice, reduced to
fourteen lines, carefully *composed* with a view to a final and over-
whelming effect... '[15]

It would seem that Valéry had been particularly struck by a
sentence near the beginning of Poe's essay where, having declared
his intention to demonstrate the nature of the poetic process from
the method he himself had employed in the composition of 'The
Raven', Poe continues:

'It is my design to render it manifest that no one point in its
composition is referable either to accident or intuition – that the
work proceeded, step by step, to its completion with the precision
and rigid consequence of a mathematical problem.'

We know now that Poe was not very sincere, or even truthful,
in what he wrote about his own compositions. He was a skilful
plagiarist and had good reason for disowning the visitations of
the Muse. As for Valéry, though he was to remain addicted to the

mathematical analogy, to the pretence of a *science* of poetics, he nevertheless elaborated the scientific analogy in a very unscientific manner:

'We must despair of a clear vision in these matters. One must lull oneself with an image. My image of the poet is of a mind full of resources and cunning, feigning sleep at the imaginary centre of his yet uncreated work, the better to await that instant of his own power which is his prey. In the vague depths of his eyes all the forces of his desire, all the springs of his instinct are taut. And there, waiting for the chance events from which she selects her food – there, most obscure in the middle of the webs and the secret harps which she had fashioned from language, whose threads are interwoven and always vaguely vibrating – a mysterious Arachne, huntress muse, is on the watch.'[16]

The Muse, as it were, comes in by the back door; and to her, surprisingly, Valéry gives the name of the Self. Here is what is perhaps the key to his final statement of the problem, from his essay 'Concerning *Le Cimetiére marin*' (1933):

'I enjoy work only as work: beginnings bore me, and I suspect everything that comes at the first attempt of being capable of improvement. Spontaneity, even when excellent or seductive, has never seemed to me sufficiently *mine*. I do not say that "I am right", but that is how I am. . . . The notion of Myself is no simpler than that of Author: a further degree of consciousness opposes a new *Self* to a new *Other*.'[17]

Valéry developed this distinction still further in a later essay – 'Poetry and Abstract Thought' (1939), pointing to the difference that exists between our *sensibility as a whole* and the faculty with which we elaborate a work of art. He quotes the well-known interchange between Mallarmé and Degas ('My dear Degas, one does not make poetry with ideas, but with *words*.') and says that Mallarmé was right. 'But when Degas spoke of ideas', he continues, 'he was, after all, thinking of inner speech or of images, which might have been expressed in *words*. But these words, these secret phrases which he called ideas, all these intentions and perceptions of the mind, do not make verses. There is something else, then, a modification, or a transformation, sudden or not, spontaneous or not, laborious or not, which must necessarily intervene between the thought that produces ideas – that activity and multiplicity of inner questions and solutions – and, on the other hand, that discourse, so different from ordinary speech, which is verse, which is so curiously ordered, which answers no need *unless it be the need it must itself create*, which never speaks but of absent things or of things profoundly and secretly felt: strange discourse, as though made by someone *other* than the speaker and addressed to someone *other* than the listener. In short, it is a *language within a language*.'[18]

We are a long way from the ideal of a composition proceeding to its completion with the precision and rigid consequence of a mathematical problem which Valéry had accepted as an ideal fifty years earlier. Valéry's long tussle with words and meanings had taught him that the 'state of poetry' is 'completely irregular, inconstant, involuntary, and fragile, and that we lose it, as we find it, *by accident*'. But the same experience had also taught him (and in this he remained faithful to Poe) that inspiration is a private affair. The poet does not become a poet until he has created the state of poetry in others. A world of difference exists between the poetic state or emotion, even when this is creative and original, and the production of a work of art.

More than once in the course of his critical expositions Valéry illustrates his meaning by an anecdote from his own experience. On one occasion as he went along the street where he lived he was suddenly *gripped* by a rhythm that took possession of him and soon gave him the impression of some force outside himself. 'It was as though someone else were making use of my *living-machine*. Then another rhythm overtook and combined with the first, and certain strange *transverse* relations were set up between these two principles. . . . They combined the movement of my legs and some kind of song I was murmuring, or rather which was being murmured *through me*. This composition became more and more complicated and soon in its complexity went far beyond anything I could reasonably produce with my ordinary, usable, rhythmic faculties. The sense of strangeness that I mentioned became almost painful, almost disquieting.'[19]

This rhythmical excitement was generated by the poet's 'sensibility as a whole', but that is not the point. It may be that such states are induced occasionally in all of us: the poet is the exceptional individual who can make use of such states in a practical way, the way of versification.

In Valéry's poetics we find in fact almost a reversal of the traditional conception of the Muse. In the classical conception the poet was content to be a passive instrument, the temporary channel of some kind of supernatural communication. The poet is forced to say to himself: 'In your works, my dear poet, what is good is not by you, and what is bad is indisputably yours.' In Valéry's theory there is 'a special quality, a kind of individual *energy* proper to the poet. It appears to him and reveals him to himself at certain infinitely precious moments. But these are only moments, and this higher energy . . . *exists and can act only in brief fortuitous manifestations.*'[20] And to sum up, Valéry suggests that 'certain instincts betray to us the depths where the best of us is found, but in pieces embedded in shapeless matter, odd or rough in appearance. We must separate these elements of noble metal from the mass, and take care to fuse them together and fashion some ornament.'[21] In other words, the Muse is very unreliable, and what she offers is a fitful illumination of the mysteries of life. 'Form alone exists – only form preserves the works of the mind' – an assertion which Valéry quotes from Mistral – and form is an object or event of the senses, shaped by the imagination.

Nevertheless, in all this speculation on the nature of the poetic activity, from Plato to Valéry, there is the sense of some *self* 'miraculously superior to Myself'. The poet's consciousness is in some sense divided, and can *in some sense* maintain separate activities. But occasionally a bridge is thrown across the dividing gulf, and at that unexpected moment a transformation takes place.

For some reason this transformation is not a private emotion, confined to the self, but the triumph of life in a universe of things.

2

What is this Soul then? Whence
Came it? It does not seem my own, and I
Have no self-passion or identity.
KEATS, ENDYMION, IV, 475

What we have so far been discussing is the problem of knowledge and inspiration in relation to the self, and we find ourselves involved in a paradox which has been formulated thus: 'In the moment of knowing, which is also the real moment of poetic creation, the knower ceases to exist as subject at all; and, conversely, when he comes fully to himself, as subject, he ceases to know.'[22] We have seen that this paradox was personified in myth as the poet's Muse, an archetypal figure representing the memory present to the mind in that state of consciousness we call inspiration; a memory that fades immediately we become conscious as a self of the *self*. Let us now delve a little more deeply into the psychology of this distinction, with special reference to the poetic process.

The greater part of the subject-matter of psychology is devoted to a seemingly endless discussion of the nature of consciousness, the validity of the subjective-objective distinction in thought, and to the problem of knowledge in general. I must try not to get lost in this academic wilderness. My object is the limited one of trying to define the conditions under which consciousness, as expressed in words, takes on that particular kind of concreteness we call poetic; and incidentally to distinguish this particular kind of concreteness in poetry from other kinds of verbal expression.

I know, from personal experience supported by the evidence of other poets, that in the rare moments when I am writing poetry, I am in a 'state of mind' totally distinct from the state of mind in which I composed this essay; totally distinct, too, from the state of mind in which I go about my practical activities while awake – that is to say, while conscious.[23] I am not so sure that the poetic state differs essentially from my state of mind when I am asleep and dreaming, but as soon as I become conscious I forget my dream, and even if, on rare occasions, I can recall my dream, it is in a state of mind now distinct from the state of my mind in the act of dreaming. I think we must leave the dreaming mind on one side; it may offer analogies to the state of mind in poetic creation, but since writing a poem is an activity of which the poet is conscious, the dreaming mind is divided from the creative mind by the very faculty we wish to investigate – *presence* of mind. – It is presence of mind, by which phrase I think we mean an awareness that the mind *is* functioning purposively, that distinguishes a genuine creative activity from a mere *afflatus*. Here one must guard oneself against a cultural priggishness. The mind is present in the writing of a good ballad or a good popular song: it is the mind that makes it 'good' rather than crude or sentimental. But 'presence' of mind does not mean consciousness of a self that thinks – indeed, it means rather the absence of any ambiguity, particularly of any confusion between conscious thought and subjective feeling. In writing a poem there is not a stream of feeling carrying words in a pre-determined direction: rather there is an autonomous verbal activity trying to establish a concrete form, a distinct existence, which may afterwards be identified (by the poet or the reader) with a feeling or state of mind. It would be paradoxical but nearer the truth to say that a verbal activity succeeds in presenting to the mind a self which the poet afterwards gratefully accepts as his own. A good poet is a stranger to the self he meets in his poetry.

   This suggests that before proceeding any farther we should try to define the self. In common usage this ubiquitous word means the rather indistinct entity present to introspection: to make ourselves aware of the characteristics of our self we have to indulge in 'self-examination'. Phrases like 'I am not feeling myself today', or 'I was beside myself with rage', show that the self is something that tends to play hide-and-seek with consciousness – presence of a self is not identical with presence of mind.

To define the 'self' has been one of the main preoccupations of modern psychology, certainly one of Jung's main preoccupations. One of Dr Jung's last works has the title *The Undiscovered Self*. But Jung found it necessary to use this word in two distinct senses, sometimes distinguishing one of them by a capital letter.

Psycho-analysis, as a theory and a therapy, rests on the hypothesis of a divided mind – part conscious, part unconscious. These two divisions of the mind are not necessarily in opposition to each other – Jung preferred to call their relation 'compensatory'. They complement one another to form a totality, which Jung called the *self*. Though the ideal presented by psycho-analysis is one of unity or integration, or at any rate of equilibrium, it is impossible, as Jung says, 'to form a clear picture of what we are as a self, for in this operation the part would have to comprehend the whole. There is little hope of our ever being able to reach even approximate consciousness of the self, since however much we may make conscious there will always exist an indeterminate and indeterminable amount of unconscious material which belongs to the totality of the self.'[24]

Jung believed that the unconscious part of the self contains all the forces that are necessary for the self-regulation of the psyche as a whole. The more we succeed in bringing into the open the personal motivations that are hidden in the unconscious, the more we shall be able to recognize these motivations for what they are (we say 'selfish') and as a consequence participate freely in the wider world of objective interests. This 'wider consciousness' is defined as 'a function of relationship to the world of objects, bringing the individual into absolute, binding, and indissoluble communion with the world at large'.[25]

Jung then introduces a further distinction – that between the *persona*, the ideal picture of a man as he thinks he should be, and the *anima*, the unconscious feminine reaction within the unconscious to this heroic concept. (In the woman the unconscious masculine reaction is called the *animus*.) In normal life a man's

anima is often projected, with the result that the hero, as Jung
says, comes under the heel of his wife's slipper. But sometimes –
and this is where the hypothesis becomes of significance for our
present purposes – sometimes the *anima* is transformed into an
intermediary between the conscious and the unconscious.
'Through this process', writes Jung, 'the *anima* forfeits the demonic
power of an autonomous complex; she can no longer exercise
the power of possession, since she is depotentiated. She is no
longer the guardian of treasures unknown; no longer Kundry,
demonic messenger of the Grail, half divine and half-animal; no
longer the soul to be called "Mistress", but a psychological
function of an intuitive nature, akin to what the primitives mean
when they say, "He has gone to the forest to talk with the spirits"
or "My snake spoke with me" or, in the mythological language
of infancy, "A little bird told me".'[26]

It is true that in this passage Jung does not mention the poet's
Muse, but the application is inescapable. One might say that in
every version of the Muse, classical and modern, she is unmistakably a *mana*-personality, 'a being of some occult and bewitching
quality (*mana*), endowed with magical knowledge and power'.

Though in a parenthesis Jung identifies the *mana*-possessed
anima with 'the artistic temperament', he proceeds to deal with
possession as evidenced in those whom he calls 'unpoetical folk'.
And he is not altogether happy about the result. The ego becomes
a *mana*-personality. 'The masculine collective figure who now
rises out of the dark background and takes possession of the
conscious personality entails a psychic danger of a subtle nature,
for by inflating the conscious mind it can destroy everything that
was gained by coming to terms with the *anima*.' The ego becomes
'inflated', and is in danger of delusions of superhuman power.
What *is* desirable – and this is what Jung meant by 'integration'
– is the achievement of a 'mid-point' of the personality, 'that
infallible something between the opposites, or else that which
unites them, or the result of conflict, or the product of energic
tension, the coming to birth of personality, a profoundly
individual step forward, the next stage'.[27]

I would like the reader to hold on to this well-known concept *mana*, as manifested in the *anima* phenomenon, for it is undoubtedly the force we are looking for, the power of inspiration in poetry and all other creative arts. Our problem is to try to discover and describe its creative process, its mode of operation. This process may not accord with the psychologist's aim, which is not to make poets of us all, but balanced personalities. As Jung says, 'the immediate goal of the analysis of the unconscious . . . is to reach a state where the unconscious contents (of the mind) no longer remain unconscious and no longer express themselves indirectly as *animus* and *anima* phenomena; that is to say, a state in which *animus* and *anima* become functions of relationship to the unconscious. So long as they are not this, they are autonomous complexes, disturbing factors that disrupt conscious control and act like true "disturbers of the peace".'[28] To use the word Jung invented, they becomes 'complexes', and the more complexes a man has, the more he may be said to be possessed; and when we try to form a picture of the personality which expresses itself through its complexes we must admit (says Jung) that 'it resembles nothing so much as an hysterical woman – i.e. the *anima!*' Which corresponds to Plato's description of the poet as a man seized with the Bacchic transport, as one possessed. When a man has got to the roots of his complexes, and in this way rid himself of his possession, Jung says that the *anima* phenomenon comes to a stop. Which is to say, the poet ceases to be poetic.

But Jung then admits that this is merely the logic of the situation. In certain cases the *mana* remains at the disposal of the ego, and then you get your supermen, your geniuses. He mentions Napoleon and Lao Tzu, but he might have mentioned Shakespeare or Goethe. Such people are to be called *mana*-personalities, and they represent an archetype that has taken shape in the human psyche: the hero, the priest and (though Jung does not say so in this particular context) the poet. The question that remains is how do these exceptional people control the flow of their *mana*: how do they avoid falling victims to its destructive forces? What powers in the ego mediate between possession and self-possession?

Jung's answer is: by means of the *self*, a 'something' 'poised between two world-pictures and their darkly discerned potentialities', 'something' that is 'strange to us and yet so near, wholly ourselves and yet unknowable, a virtual centre of so mysterious a constitution that it can claim anything – kinship with beasts and gods, with crystals and with stars – without moving us to wonder, without even exciting our disapprobation', a voice that 'it is surely wiser to listen to'.[29]

Admittedly the self is no more than a psychological concept, 'a construct that serves to express an unknowable essence which we cannot grasp as such, since by definition it transcends our power of comprehension'. It will not appeal, therefore, to the scientific mind, but neither, for that matter, does poetry, which also transcends the scientist's powers of comprehension. But as a psychological concept the self does offer a reasonable explanation of those processes of poetic inspiration and creation which hitherto have found expression only in mythological terms. It may be said that in substituting psychology for mythology we are merely substituting one kind of picture-language for another kind of picture-language. That should not deter us: the self has no known limits and art has no known limits, and to discuss their relationship is inevitably to indulge in speculation.

Our aim is nevertheless practical, and what is produced by the poet is something concrete, a poem. I think we must therefore pursue our enquiry a little further, to ask by what process does a man possessed produce an object or event of the senses that is *concrete*, 'the form alone which commands and survives' (Valéry). If we identify (as I think we must) the Muse with the *anima*, how does this Muse mediate between the demonic power at her command and the order or equilibrium upon which the self depends for its existence? The tutelary Muse 'governs' the Poet's song so that the form commands the assent of an audience, creates in them a 'state of poetry'. It is not such a mystery that we are capable of dreaming or day-dreaming: but by what means does such a fortuitous activity become purposive and effective?

Jung says that it is very difficult for a man to distinguish himself from his *anima*, but that seems to be precisely what the Poet does in the act of composition. To appreciate this fact we must return to the difficult concept of consciousness.

Again I must renounce any attempt to define consciousness – psychology, as a subject, has been concerned with little else, and its conclusions are in the main negative. It may be that the immediate content of consciousness is 'always a particular state of the brain',[30] but long ago William James showed that even this elementary fact could not be asserted with any sureness. 'Whenever I try to become sensible of my thinking activity as such, what I catch is some bodily fact, an impression coming from my brow, or head, or throat, or nose. It seems as if consciousness as an inner activity were rather a *postulate* than a sensibly given fact, the postulate, namely, of a *knower* as correlative to all this known . . .'[31] His statement, at the conclusion of his *Psychology*, that psychology consists of a 'string of raw facts; a little gossip and wrangle about opinions; a little classification and generalization on the mere descriptive level; a strong prejudice that we *have* states of mind, and that our brain conditions them: but not a single law in the sense in which physics show us laws, not a single proposition from which any consequence can causally be deduced' – all this remains true seventy or more years since James wrote the words. Almost exactly two centuries earlier John Locke had defined consciousness as 'the perception of what passes in a man's own mind'; that is to say, the presence of the self to itself, the ground of personal identity. This remained the accepted notion of consciousness until James pointed out that consciousness is not static, but a process in time – he described it as a 'stream', a metaphor that was to have incalculable consequences for psychology and for art. James was already aware that 'states of mind' are by no means clearly apprehensible if distinguished from their objects – consciousness is always consciousness *of something* – 'the thoughts themselves are the thinkers' . . . 'it thinks'. Phenomenology is a philosophy based on the presumed identity of consciousness and object. Existentialism is an attempt to objectify the self so that it can become an object of consciousness

– we dam the stream with barriers to make us aware of its flow. The most effective of such barriers are works of art. A work of art is a moment of arrest in the stream of consciousness: a feature of the work of art that distressed Bergson.[32] The artist has no philosophical doubts: his difficulty is to arrest the stream at a significant moment. This 'moment' we can call an 'image'.

Consciousness, says Sartre, is always intentional. That is to say, we become conscious of an object in the course of an action, in order to situate that object in our pursuit of Being. Consciousness is therefore a creative (or perhaps one could say a 'concretive') activity – without consciousness there would not be a world, mountains, rivers, tables, chairs, etc.; there would be *only* Being. In this sense *there is no thing* without consciousness, but there is not *Nothing*. Consciousness causes *there to be* things because it is itself nothing. Only through consciousness is there differentiation, meaning, and plurality for 'Being'.[33]

As I have said, I want to avoid getting lost in these definitions of consciousness. I shall try therefore to confine myself to what I believe to be a very practical problem – the corruption of consciousness that results in bad art. This corruption is the key, not only to the distortion and loss of inspiration in the individual artist, but also to the decline of art in a civilization – and therefore, consequently, to the decline of that civilization. And that is the point of my argument: corruption of consciousness takes place when the Poet abandons his Muse.

A young philospher, with whom I generally find myself in complete sympathy, has pointed out that the basic premise of existentialist as opposed to classical thinking is 'that truth is those arrangements or patterns of things which man as a purposeful activity has brought into being and which is therefore accessible to *consciousness* and which need not be sought out by reason'.[34] The key word in this definition is 'things' – things brought into being and *therefore* made accessible to consciousness. There is no consciousness without things and consciousness may therefore be described as a process of reification – a making of 'things' by virtue of which we become conscious. If we can imagine a world without things in which nevertheless human beings existed, such human beings would be without consciousness, unconscious.

The world is, however, 'full of a number of things' and these enter into consciousness by the normal process of perception. But things 'out of this world', as we say – feelings, emotions, intuitions, etc. – are only brought into consciousness in the degree that they are reified, i.e. given 'thingly' or concrete existence. The process of making things is, as Vico was the first to point out, art: art is the creation of things which therewith become accessible to consciousness. We do not normally call everything that we make a work of art: many things we make are merely replicas of existing things, and familiarity with things breeds an unawareness of their existence. But when we make a new thing to stand for a feeling, emotion or intuition hitherto unexpressed, then we make a work of art. An unreified feeling is what Valéry calls the poetic state of mind and a poem is a thing that stands for this state of mind. The world might therefore be said to consist of poetry and prose, of things and their replicas.

William James has a vivid image which beautifully illustrates this distinction. 'When we take a general view of the wonderful stream of our consciousness, what strikes us first is the different pace of its parts. Like a bird's life, it seems to be an alternation of flights and perchings. The rhythm of language expresses this, where every thought is expressed in a sentence, and every sentence closed by a period. The resting places are usually occupied by sensorial imaginations of some sort, whose peculiarity is that they can be held before the mind for infinite time, and contemplated without changing; the places of flight are filled with thoughts of relations, static or dynamic, that for the most part obtain between the matters contemplated in the periods of comparative rest. *Let us call the resting-places the "substantive parts", and the places of flight the "transitive parts" of the stream of thought.*'[35]

Without realizing that he had done so, James in this paragraph has defined the essence of the work of art – it is a resting-place in the stream of consciousness, which was also Bergson's definition of a work of art. But James goes on to point out that in normal

processes of thought it is very difficult to see the 'transitive' parts
for what they really are. 'Our thinking tends at all times towards
some other substantive part than the one from which it has just
been dislodged.' But equally, in normal processes of thought, it
is very difficult to linger on the perch: not only is the rush of
thought so headlong that it almost brings us up at the conclusion
before we can arrest it (James); or if we are nimble enough and
do arrest it, then, says James, it ceases to be itself. 'As a snowflake
crystal in the warm hand is no longer a crystal but a drop, so,
instead of catching the feeling of relation moving to its term, we
find we have caught some substantive thing, usually the last word
we were pronouncing, statically taken, and with its function,
tendency, and particular meaning in the sentence quite evapo-
rated.' But suppose that we could catch that substantive thing,
supposing that the snowflake in all its crystalline perfection of
form were to remain unchanged in our warm hand – why, then
we should have caught a thing of beauty and a joy for ever: a
work of art!

There would be many qualifications to make about such a metaphysical representation of the poetic process, some of which
James himself makes when refuting what he calls 'the ridiculous
theory of Hume and Berkeley that we can have no images but of
perfectly definite things'. It is true that there was a school of
poets which strove to hold on to the image in all its pristine
precision – they were called the Imagists and I belonged to it.
But the attempt was vain because, as James says, 'every definite
image in the mind is steeped and dyed in the free water that
flows round it. With it goes the sense of its relations, near and
remote, the dying echo of whence it came to us, the dawning
sense of whither it is to lead. The significance, the value, of the
image is all in this halo or penumbra that surrounds and escorts
it – or rather that is fused into one with it and has become bone
of its bone and flesh of its flesh; leaving it, it is true, an image of
the same *thing* it was before, but making it an image of that thing
newly taken and freshly understood.'[36]

Armed with these psychological insights let us now return to

Valéry's conception of the faculty with which we elaborate a work of art, 'a kind of energy proper to the poet', and let us see whether we are now in a position to account for the persisting myth of a poet's Muse.

We have seen that modern psychology has disintegrated the notion of an all-knowing, self-knowing self. This disintegration is an empirical fact, and when, as in Jung's psychology, we speak of the re-integration, or 'individuation', of the personality, we are expressing an ideal of some sort, a state of mental equilibrium, desirable perhaps from the point of view of sanity or morality, but not necessarily consistent with the 'Bacchic transport' of a poet, with the experience of inspiration. It may be that from the point of view of the poet's audience the experience of poetry is desirable as catharsis: that was Aristotle's point of view, and it implies, as we have seen, that we must carefully distinguish between the process of poetry and its effects. For the moment we are concerned only with the process, with the creative self and not with the ideal social self. I am inclined to the hypothesis that there is a self that flies and a self that perches, and that the work of art is the state of consciousness at the moment of perching, the resting-place itself and therefore something distinct from the flight, from the so-called stream of consciousness. I call this resting-place the *image*, but only on the understanding that we define the image in concrete terms, and distinguish it clearly from what philosophers call universals or ideas. Art is an awareness of the particularity of particular things – I think all philosophers of art from Plato to Coleridge and Collingwood have said something of the kind. Particulars are bright points of vision precipitated by the stream of consciousness, and to the degree that these bright points are held in suspension, a 'Heraclitean fire' (to use Gerard Manley Hopkins's phrase) redeemed from the flux, to that extent (even if they are no more than a verbal image or a musical chord) they are works of art. The poet is the redeemer of words from the 'free flow'– words which may nevertheless be steeped in associations.

Since the immediate data of a state of consciousness correspond with a state of the brain, we must ask what trigger mechanism releases any particular image from the brain and sends it into the stream of consciousness. To this we can only reply that it must be an intensification of feeling, which results in an apperception of value: a vague feeling-tone becomes concrete, acquires direction and is precipitated into consciousness as an image. But the odd thing is that the image, like the snow-crystal, enters consciousness fully formed, effective by reason of its form. What agency, behind consciousness, has had this formative function? That is the final and most significant question.

Valéry, in one of his dialogues, asks the same question through the mouth of Socrates: 'If some Reason were to dream, standing hard, erect, her eyes armed, mouth shut, mistress of her lips – would not her dream be what we are now looking at – this world of measured forces and studied illusions? – A dream, a dream, but all charged with symmetries, all order, all acts, all sequences! . . .Who can tell what august Laws are here dreaming that they have clothed their faces with brightness and agreed to make manifest to mortals how the real, the unreal, and the intelligible can fuse and combine, obedient to the Muses?'[37]

If Reason herself were to dream 'a dream of vigilance and tension'– there we have the hypothesis we need! But can we translate such a concept into psychological terms?

I think we can if we assume that the brain is not merely a store-house of buried impressions (of psycho-physical correspondences) but also a system of molecular structure. We assume that the brain is a system of physical molecules, but I think we must suppose that it is also a system of mental facts or monads – that the infinite store of impressions fed into the brain by sensations is auto-matically sorted into *Gestalten*, metaphysical configurations of infinite significance and viability. If I am told that there is no empirical evidence of such a process taking place, I can only reply that perception itself is precisely this process: it is the internal 'requiredness' thanks to which, according to the *Gestalt* psycho-logists, a coherent vision of the external world is possible. A work of art, as Koffka has said, is not an idle play of the emotions, but a means of helping us to find our place in the world –'in a universe that is infinitely greater than our egos'. Or, as the same psychologist puts it, in a work of art 'mere factuality is subordinated to requiredness'.[38]

We thus finally come to identify the Muse with Reason – with a Reason that dreams in measure and order, in symmetry and rhythm. But the dream visits the consciousness of the poet – is perhaps called to that consciousness by the blind necessities of feeling or emotion. In that case why are not all our minds immaculate screens waiting for the impress of the Muse's images? – or, to use Plato's metaphor, why are they not all blocks of wax of the right consistency? Why are great poets such rare mortals?

Because, I would suggest, our mental screens are for the most part neither pure nor luminous. Most of us suffer from a corrupt, one might even say a defiled, consciousness. We have lost 'the innocent eye', the inner eye of direct or primitive sensation. We realize this whenever we look at the world through a child's eyes, as recorded in the paintings and poems of children. We realize it too, whenever we look at the world through the eyes of a so-called 'savage' (who is not so savage as we who conspire to destroy the human race), the savage for whom the image is more real than the phenomenal object, the dream more real than deliberate action, or more real than the purposive thought that leads to deliberate action. In effect there are two stages in 'becoming conscious' of something, first the image, then the idea – first we look at the burning coal, then we see the colour red. Generally speaking we distinguish between sensation and imagination, but we do not often realize that imagination can be concrete – Goethe defined art as the faculty of exact sensuous imagination.[39]

This distinction is of profound significance for the theory of art, as perhaps among philosophers only Collingwood has realized. He pointed out that consciousness has a double object where sentience has a single one. 'What we hear, for example, is merely sound. What we attend to is two things at once: a sound and an act of hearing it. The act of sensation is not present to itself, but it is present, together with its own sensum, to the act of attention. This is, in fact, the special significance of the *con-* in the word consciousness: it indicates a togetherness of the two things, sensation and sensum, both of which are present to the conscious mind.'[40] It follows that when we pass from sentience to an act of attention, of awareness or consciousness, the impression has changed into an idea and a new principle is established. 'Attention is focussed on one thing to the exclusion of the rest. . . . Consciousness, master in its own house, dominates feeling.' And at this moment (the moment to recall James's metaphor of rest on the perch) feeling takes *form*. Collingwood actually uses words which seem to echo William James: 'Attending to a feeling means holding it before the mind; rescuing it from the flux of mere sensation, and conserving it for so long as may be necessary in order that we may take note of it' – in order, I would say, that we can have an image of it.

We must, if we are poets, hold on to this precision of the process of fixation. Consciousness, as Collingwood points out, is a level of thought that is not yet intellect. 'Consciousness is thought in its absolutely fundamental and original shape.' In that shape it does not always meet with the approval of the intellect. The intellect, the ego of the psycho-analysts, then becomes a censor of the imagination and from this fact results that corruption of consciousness which is not only an abortion of poetic feeling, but a disease of the mind that eventually leads to the corruption of language and the decline of a civilization.[41]

I am not trying (and certainly Collingwood would not have condoned such an attempt) to identify imagination with sensation or art with feeling: between the feeling and the work of art there is a force (*mana:* the 'energy proper to the poet') which fuses the impressions of sense into formal and significant images. Collingwood says that in attending to a present feeling consciousness perpetuates that feeling. But only by giving it form, by creating a clear and distinct image. Such images, in their purity, are the primary elements in poetry and in all the arts.

When we say, as Collingwood and William James say, that consciousness is 'absolutely autonomous',[42] we are really saying that the mind is divided into two fields – 'a background or penumbra from which attention is withdrawn' (Collingwood) and an object of attention – the distinction between hearing and listening, between seeing and looking. The poet's creative mind is equally divided between sensation and attention – between hearing and seeing on the one hand and looking and listening on the other. His sensations he cannot control – they enter consciousness as 'brain states', 'patterns of electrical impulses, or electrical fields, of great complexity'.[43] But then they are shaped by a distinct force, the energy proper to the poet, Coleridge's 'shaping power of the imagination'. The Muse is clearly an archetypal figure conceived at the dawn of civilization to represent this shaping power, and such an archetype is still serviceable for a modern theory of poetry, for an adequate philosophy of art. Whence the Muse's power proceeds we must leave as a biological mystery – it is the *mana* we identify with the source of life itself, which is formative in its deepest recesses. To the extent that we allow our sensibility to be guided by this shaping power, this 'dream of vigilance and tension', and exclude all judgements and prejudices proceeding from the ego (which Plato called 'the lie in the soul'[44]) to that extent we are true poets and worthy to receive the truth revealed by the Muse.

VII

The Biological Significance of Art

There is an early story of Tolstoy's, which has always seemed to me to to have a fundamental bearing on the relation of the creative activities we call 'art' to the destructive forces we call 'crime'. Tolstoy describes a walk he took with three boys from the school on his estate at Yásnaya Polyána. In class they had been excited by the reading of a violent story by Gogol. It was a moonless winter night with snow on the ground and clouds in the sky. In a spirit of daring the boys wanted to go into the woods where wolves prowled but, being too afraid, they skirted round them, and began to talk about Caucasian robbers. Tolstoy told them tales about the Cossack braves he had known when he was a soldier, and particularly about one who, when surrounded by his enemies, broke out into song and threw himself on his dagger. The children were struck by the strange fact that a man should sing when he was about to die. But their appetite for horrors was not satisfied, so Tolstoy went on to recount the gruesome murder of his aunt, whose throat had been cut by robbers. They stopped in a thicket at the end of the village, and Tolstoy, with his acute eye for significant detail, describes how one of the children picked up a dry stick from the snow and began striking it against the frosty trunk of a lime tree. Hoar frost fell from the branches on to their caps and the noise of the

Saturday Evening Post, Philadelphia, 26 September 1959

blows resounded in the stillness of the wood. Then another of the children, Fédka, a boy of ten 'with a tender, receptive, poetic yet daring nature', suddenly asked: 'Why does one learn singing? I often think, why, really, does one?' Tolstoy comments: 'What made him jump from the terror of the murder to this question, heaven only knows; yet by the tone of his voice, the seriousness with which he demanded an answer, and the attentive silence of the other two, one felt there was some vital and legitimate connection between this question and our preceding talk. Whether the connection lay in some response to my suggestion that crime might be explained by lack of education (I had spoken of that), or whether he was testing himself – transferring himself into the mind of the murderer and remembering his own favourite occupation (he has a wonderful voice and immense musical talent), or whether the connection lay in the fact that he felt that now was the time for sincere conversation, and all the problems demanding solution rose in his mind – at any rate his question surprised none of us.'

'And what is drawing for? And why write well?' Tolstoy asked, not knowing how to answer the child's question. 'What is drawing for?' repeated Fédka, and Tolstoy adds: 'He was really asking, What is Art for? And I could not explain.'

Tolstoy thought about this question all his life, and it was not until thirty-seven years later, in his book *What is Art?* that he tried to explain the mysterious relationship that exists between beauty and truth, between art and life.[1]

Tolstoy knew that the relationship was very profound, and even these children knew instinctively that there is some intimate connection between beauty and violence, between love and death. Such a connection is made by the great poets, by Homer and the Greek tragedians, by Shakespeare and by Tolstoy himself in *War and Peace*, but now we have lost it. Our technological civilization ignores all such values in its blind drive towards power and affluence, and pays the toll in a mass neurosis whose symptoms are fearful despair, apathy and violence.

In recent years violence has increased, especially among young people. Sometimes it seems to be motivated by race prejudice, not only in countries like the United States and South Africa where there is an indigenous and long-persisting racial problem, but even in Great Britain – we may recall the riots in London and Nottingham a few years ago when coloured immigrants from the West Indies were beaten up and their homes smashed. This outbreak seems to have had little to do with racial prejudice. Colour was only an excuse to exercize an impulse which would, if necessary, have found other outlets. The teen-age delinquent and, at a more literate level, the Angry Young Man, are giving vent to suppressed feelings of frustration. Something in their nature has no disciplined outlet, and in their boredom and restless urge to action, these frustrated youths seek to hurt, to destroy; for destruction, as Bakunin said, is also creation. More exactly, it is a substitute for creation.

Such violence of action is no doubt related to the violence of expression that has increasingly become a feature, not only of novels, newspapers, films and television, but also of literature universally acclaimed as of great cultural value. America is not unique in this respect; the cynical brutality of William Faulkner's novels, for example, is but an outstanding example of a phenomenon characteristic of our civilization everywhere.

Violence, of course, is not new to literature. There is violence in the *Iliad* and the epic generally is a celebration of mutual slaughter among men. There is violence in Shakespeare and Cervantes, but the violence is never condoned by these writers. They view it as just retribution for sins against the divine order, or as a sacrifice sanctioned by heroism or martyrdom. What is peculiar to modern literature is violence for the sake of violence, gratuitous violence. Perhaps our reverence for life has been dulled by mass slaughter, though mass slaughter has not been exceptional in the history of mankind. What is exceptional is the boredom that now alternates with war. The basic emotion in peacetime has become a *horror vacui*: a fear of being alone, of having nothing to do, a neurosis whose symptoms are restlessness, an unmotivated and undirected rage, sinking at times into vapid listlessness. This neurotic fear in the individual is intensified by the prevailing sense of insecurity. We do not consciously think about the threat of atomic war, but it has corrupted our faith in life itself, and given poignancy to our moods of boredom.

This universal neurosis has developed step by step with the technological development of our civilization. It is the neurosis of men whose sole expenditure of energy is to pull a lever, or push a button, of men who have ceased to make things with their hands, even to transport themselves with their legs. Such inactivity is a cessation not only of the muscular exercises and nervous combinations that constituted the normal life of man before the technological revolution; it is also a cessation of those formative or creative mental processes that even at the level of simple craft operations or manual tasks, engaged the will in a positive and productive action. If one could contrast visually, in the manner of the time-and-motion studies of the sociologists, the daily actions of an eighteenth-century chairmaker and those of a twentieth-century machinist, the latter would appear as a confined, repetitive clot, the former as a free and fantastic arabesque. But the most significant contrast could not be visualized, for it is mental: the contrast between a mind suspended aimlessly above an autonomous movement, and a mind consciously bent on the shaping of a material substance according to the persistent evidence of the senses.

Routine activities existed in other ages, but generally speaking, human beings were in direct contact with nature and dependent on *things*. It was a realization of this fact which caused Jean-Jacques Rousseau, long before the Industrial Revolution, to lay down as one of the first principles of education: *Keep the child dependent on things only*. Rousseau believed that the child learns by trial and error better than by formula. This kind of pragmatic learning is essentially physical; skill develops in coping with material objects. It is true that skill of this kind is still involved in many industrial processes; we still divide labour into skilled and unskilled categories. But too often today skill means the understanding and control of a mechanical process, rather than the manual shaping of a physical substance. It is an activity more cerebral than sensual. This is true even of agricultural operations; the peasant who formerly used the spade and the scythe has been replaced by a mechanic driving a tractor.

Sport also still implies skill in the physical sense, but the increasing professionalism of games confines the physical effects of such activities to a very small number of people. Sport, too, has become a mental activity.

I know of no detailed study of the universal cerebralization of productive activities that has taken place in all advanced technological civilizations during the past century and a half, and that has increased in intensity during the past fifty years. But such a change in the basic modes of human activity must have deeply affected mental life and moral behaviour. The most obvious expression of such a change might well be aimlessly aggressive. Satan always finds some mischief still for idle hands to do. Unused energies, deprived of traditional or habitual outlets, explode in violence.

I have spoken of 'skill', a word of Norse derivation whose original meaning implied discrimination. It is a curious fact that the word has no equivalent in French or German. The nearest equivalent in French is *habilité*, which is not the same thing. The German *Geschicktlichkeit* means 'giftedness'; *Fertigkeit* means 'readiness'. We use 'skill' in association with 'craft', an old English word that originally meant power or strength. The association of craft with words like skill, art or occupation exists in English only: a skilled craftsman is a worker with the power of discrimination. 'Know-how' is a popular equivalent.

The Greeks, though the source of our philosophy of art, had no word for art. They used *technē* – the equivalent of our word 'skill'. The word 'art' is derived from the Latin *ars*, which also implies skill, and this word is derived from the root *ar*, meaning to fit or join. The Romans were probably responsible for the distinction that gradually developed between arts and crafts, for they personified the Arts and began to think of them as refined (i.e. fine) activities. Nevertheless during the Middle Ages the primary meaning of art remained skill – skill in making things, whether a chair, a tapestry, a painting, a piece of music or a poem. The liberal arts taught in schools were taught as objective skills – grammar, rhetoric, logic; arithmetic, geometry, music and astronomy. We no longer speak of the liberal arts, but of *science*, that is to say, various categories of *knowledge* expressed in verifiable language. The arts were a way of 'doing', involving skill; the sciences are a way of 'knowing', implying logical consistency.

The history of words is a key to the history of ideas. We have now effected a complete divorce between the originally identical concepts of *technē* and *ars*. Technique, scientific method, skilled craft – all these terms imply intellectual know-how, and are characteristic of our technological civilization. But though moribund art schools still teach art as a skill, it is regarded more as an instinctual activity, exercized by a minority of gifted people, essentially inspirational in origin and personal in manifestation and significance. Its relevance to a technological civilization is considered marginal: an optional grace which most economies cannot afford. The controlling ideal of a technological civilization is not grace or beauty, but productive efficiency.

The Greeks did not distinguish between grace and efficiency; they considered them identical. Plato in his dialogue *Politicus* argued that statesmanship was a skill, comparable to that of the weaver (or, as we should say, an art, not a science), an intuition of Form in all things – not a tyrannical application of law. The modern philosopher does not agree with Plato. Politics he considers a science. We deliver ourselves into the remote hands of technical experts, who attempt to control our natural tendencies by means of scientific organizations.

To make a distinction between the art of government and the science of government may now seem an academic exercise, but it is part of the vital problem of distinguishing between an art and a science of life itself. I call it a *vital* problem with a precise intention, because I believe that the future welfare of mankind depends on a realization of the issues involved, and then upon a clear choice of alternatives. To say that we stand at a cross-roads of human development may be a rhetorical cliché, but it is nevertheless a formidable fact.

Let us now look more closely at this human faculty we call 'skill'. Dr Loren C. Eiseley, the distinguished American anthropologist, has suggested that skill is the faculty upon which man has depended for his survival in the struggle for existence. Man has not reached his present superior status in the evolution of species by force alone, or even by adjustment to changes in his environment. He has reached it by the development of consciousness, enabling him to discriminate the *quality* of things. To quote Dr Eiseley's own words: 'Man has become . . . a value-creating animal. He sets his own goals and more and more exerts his own will upon recalcitrant matter and the natural forces of the universe. In this activity he has passed from the specialized evolution of the parts of the body to a projection of such "part" evolution upon his machines and implements. In this respect man is a unique being. Having achieved high intellectual ability, he may remain comparatively unchanged in structure while all around him other animals are still subjected to the old laws of specialized selection.'[2]

The long historical process whereby man became able to impose his will on recalcitrant matter can be reconstructed only speculatively. But there is nothing speculative about the process through which the child achieves this capacity. It has been studied in all its intricacy by the great Swiss pedagogue Jean Piaget, who has published a whole series of books based on his patient observations of infantile behaviour. In one of them (*The Origin of Intelligence in the Child*) he defines intelligence as a relationship between the human organism and things. It is not, he insists, a power of reflection independent of the organism's particular position in the universe; rather it is linked, from the very beginning, with the organism's reaction to its physical environment. But this is not a simple reflex action; simultaneously with the organism's assimilation of external things, there is a mental organization of the things assimilated. The infant 'gropes' among its first confused experiences, becomes aware of certain relationships between the acts to be performed and an end to be attained, and *profits from experience*. Habits are formed, reactions to environment are automatically repeated, and gradually the groping becomes more continuous and consistent until it constitutes an *intention*. Intention is the essential characteristic of intelligence.

An act is intentional, according to Piaget's definition, when it is determined by re-presentation, as distinct from the elementary associations of the organism and its environment in which an act is determined by an external stimulus.

Intelligence therefore presupposes intention. Intention is connected with the power of evoking images, and eventually with the whole process of symbolization and speech. In a series of observations of sucking reflexes in infants, Piaget shows that intentional adaptation begins as soon as the child transcends the level of simple corporal activities such as sucking itself, listening, looking, grasping, and *acts upon things and uses the inter-relationships of objects*. In other words, intelligence develops (as Rousseau perceived) in contact with things, and increases in its range and capacity in so far as the images derived from this basic sensuous experience are formed and reformed in imaginative activity. (Piaget defines imagination as 'invention through mental combination'.)

Intention implies intention *towards* something. It is motivated by what Freud called the pleasure-principle, which in terms of bodily reactions is simply a sense of balance or ease. It will be seen that an element of choice is involved – a choice between the various mental combinations that might make for mental comfort. Where there is choice there is value. Value, as Piaget says, is the expression of desirability at all levels of experience, and it is my contention that the desirable values are always aesthetic – that is to say, determined by their contribution to whatever structure of experience gives the greatest pleasure to the organism. Such an ideal of equilibrium represents the final goal of our actions, and whatever means are used to attain this goal are the 'values' involved not only in life's primary processes, but also in the work of art. There is a continuous link between the methods that determine the origins of intelligence in the child and the methods that determine the beauty of a work of art.

We are still left with the problem of defining the values that make for ease and stability. There is a school of psychologists, of German origin but now active in the United States, which has concentrated on this problem – the problem of why things look the way they do. They find the solution in perception itself. Perception is a process that gives a coherent order to the jumble of images received by the senses. We *learn* to see. We learn to give these images a good layout or *Gestalt* (the German word from which the school takes its name). According to Professor Koffka, the nervous system, under the impact of the stimulations that impinge on the retina of the eyes, 'produces processes of organization in such a way that the pattern produced is the best possible under the prevailing conditions . . . thus colour and brightness, shape and space, figure and background, location and motion, are all *interdependent* aspects of the organized pattern which ordinary visual stimulation will produce'.[3] In other words, the way the nervous system develops its organized patterns is not very different from the way the artist paints his pictures. It is by this faculty of assimilating sensuous impressions from material things and then combining them in significant relationships, that the human race found its place in the world, and it is this faculty that contemporary man utilizes less and less. Mental faculties can develop only through use. Thus, the whole structure of human intelligence is now threatened at its foundations.

An infinite distance may seem to separate the sucking reflexes of an infant from the constructive intelligence needed to build a cathedral or compose a symphony, but the same laws of perception are involved. They are involved in any process of discrimination, which we have found to be the meaning of words like craft or skill. It follows that the same laws are also involved in the appreciation of a work of art, for the appreciation is based on a play of perceptual images that re-enacts the processes underlying artistic creation. An artist works towards a unity that emerges progressively from his perception and manipulation of material quantities, whereas we who appreciate the result begin with this unity and afterwards become aware of the isolated quantities which have cohered to produce it.

We enjoy works of art because they possess these values of required order and unity. But what we do not often realize is that the same formal values differentiate intelligence from sensorimotor reflexes at every stage of human mental development.

Such facts in relation to the tendencies of a technological civilization are now seen to be far-reaching and devastating. It is true that we cannot yet generalize about our whole contemporary social structure; it varies from country to country, and there are entire nations, particularly in Asia and Africa, who, though enjoying the imported products of technology, are not yet subject to its immediate impact. What I have to say, therefore, applies mainly to North America and Europe. Here, too few men have little sensuous contact with the soil, with animals, with the handling of wood, clay or metal. Progressive schools make some attempt to give the child sensuous experience. But technology is a ruthless tyranny, and its processes demand from the educational system a training directed exclusively towards conceptual modes of thought. 'Money, mechanization, algebra. The three monsters of contemporary civilization.' So wrote Simone Weil in her *Notebooks*,[4] and in another remarkable book, *The Human Condition*,[5] Hannah Arendt confirms this intuition. Earth alienation, she says, is the hallmark of modern science. 'Under the sign of earth alienation, every science, not only physical and natural science, so radically changed its innermost content that one may doubt whether prior to the modern age anything like science existed at all. This is perhaps clearest in the development of the new science's most important mental instrument, the devices of modern algebra, by which mathematics "succeeded in freeing itself from the shackles of spatiality", that is, from geometry, which, as the name indicates, depends on terrestrial measures and measurements. Modern mathematics freed man from the shackles of earth-bound experience and his power of cognition from the shackles of finitude.' Virtually all higher education in the modern world aspires to this mathematical ideal, in which direct sensuous experience is no longer admitted as evidence – in which everything is reduced to a cosmic language of abstract symbols.

But these, it will be said, are the methods by which science has won its greatest victories; to logic and mathematics, to introspection rather than observation, to hypothesis rather than classification, we owe the wonders (and the terrors) of our atomic age.

All this is true, and I shall not try to balance these achievements against the evils that have accompanied them. What is more significant is the anxiety, the all-prevailing sense of insecurity which undoubtedly motivates the crime and violence of our age.

Many earnest people call for moral sanctions. Man's ethical standards, they point out, have not kept pace with his scientific knowledge. He has lost his sense of sin, and has no fear of retribution. But our moral philosophers and religious leaders fail to indicate any practical methods for imbuing a technological civilization with ethical standards. Morality is not so much a question of beliefs as of habitual behaviour, of tradition. Moral habits are acquired in the home, in the school, in the social milieu. One might say they are conditioned reflexes, like those of a domesticated animal. No man is good simply because he believes in goodness, but because the way of life in which he was brought up is good. What incentives to goodness exist in the mechanized ways of a technological society? This is not a political question, a question of the relative moral values of socialism or capitalism: all contemporary political systems are technological. In this respect their aims and ideals are identical. Technical idealism dominates the world, and displaces all forms of moral idealism.

What we must finally recognize is the existence of two distinct modes of intelligence: one, which might be called the Cartesian intelligence since it began with Descartes, who was the first philosopher to divorce reasoning from a sensuous dependence on things (I *think*, therefore I am); and one which might be called the aesthetic intelligence since it maintains contact with the sensuous world at every stage of its reasoning (I *feel*, therefore I am: reality is a creation of my senses). To the Cartesian intelligence we owe the great structures of rational or idealistic thought; to the aesthetic intelligence the discoveries of the physical sciences and the creation of works of art. In the modern world we have never kept a sensible balance between these two modes of intelligence, and so we have reached the abyss which now separates the man of feeling from the man of thought, the geometrician from the mathematician, the practical scientist from the scientific philosopher. Higher education in the modern world aspires to an ideal of theoretical or intellectual perfection in which direct sensuous experience is no longer admitted as evidence. The only truths are logical, and they are of no practical importance.

To cultivate the aesthetic intelligence would require a complete change in the direction and ideals of education. To keep the child dependent on things only, as recommended by Rousseau, would mean a considerable sacrifice of the efforts which are now made to emancipate the child from things and make it dependent on words only, that is to say, on abstract thought. While not denying the disciplinary virtues of subjects like logic and algebra, their ideals should not be confused with those of the physical or natural sciences. Scientists like Newton and Einstein have proclaimed their dependence on the vivid imagery that comes from sensuous experience, or like Darwin have lamented a life devoted to abstractions.

Whether we are scientists or artists, our aim is what Wordsworth called 'joy in widest commonalty spread', a society rid of its neuroses, a civilization rid of the threat of annihilating war. This aim will never be achieved by political legislation or by any form of totalitarian coercion. The change must come about organically, and must correspond to those vital laws which from the moment of birth determine the physical and psychological equilibrium of unfolding life.

These laws are known. It remains only to magnify them to the scale of our social problem and to animate them with that faith in life which is the final sanction of all human endeavour. For life, in its intimate recesses, is intelligence, is skill, is art. But how shall we penetrate to these recesses and ensure that life's creative forces are liberated?

Tolstoy had an answer to this question and I believe that it is the true answer. Tolstoy was not an impractical visionary. He was a man who had experienced to the full the passions and tragedies of life. He had been a soldier and a landowner, a father and a schoolmaster, a sinner and a saint; he had possessed great riches and given all that he had to the poor; he wrote the greatest prose epic of our time and he ranks with the few greatest figures of world literature. In *What is Art?*, a mature work of his old age, he answered the questions of the schoolboy Fedká – What is art for? He answered it in three clear sentences: the evolution of feeling proceeds by means of art; art is accessible to all men; art and only art can cause violence to be set aside. 'The task of art is enormous. Through the influence of real art, aided by science, guided by religion, that peaceful co-operation of man which is now maintained by external means – by our law-courts, police, charitable institutions, factory inspection, and so forth, – should be obtained by man's free and joyous activity.'

It is not necessary to agree with everything Tolstoy said about art – he sometimes allowed moral prejudices to cloud his aesthetic judgement. But he realized as no one since Plato had so clearly realized that art is not an ornamental addition to life, 'not a pleasure, a solace, or an amusement. . . . Art is an organ of human life transmitting man's reasonable perception into feeling.' Not only is art a process or experience co-equally important with science for the life and progress of mankind, but it has the unique function of uniting men in love of each other and of life itself. Why does one learn singing? What is drawing for? Tolstoy could now answer these questions and we can now answer them. The cultivation of the art is an education of the sensibilities, and if we are not given an education of this kind, if our hands remain empty and our perception of form is unexercised, then in idleness and vacancy we revert to violence and crime. When there is no will to creation the death instinct takes over and wills endless, gratuitous destruction.

An education of the sensibilities – what I have in one of my books called an 'education through art' – is not the present concern of our schools or of adult education. Something is done at the primary stage – at kindergarten and infant schools; but the child is then quickly swallowed up in a system that ignores the evolution of feeling and provides no time for the free and joyous activity of art. To know becomes the exclusive aim of education: to create is the concern of a tiny minority that evades the social pattern of our technological civilization. The growing child gradually loses all contact with things, all capacity to manipulate materials or discriminate forms. Unless we can discover a method of basing education on these primary biological processes, not only shall we fail to create a society united in love: we shall continue to sink deeper into disunity, mass neuroses and war.

VIII

High Noon and Darkest Night

THE CONCEPT OF FORM IN THE PHILOSOPHY
OF ORTEGA Y GASSET

The revolution in art that has taken place in our time has inevitably provoked some very severe criticisms. In so far as these
are defensive of the old order, they do not normally deserve our
consideration. But occasionally, very occasionally, the criticism
of modern art is based on a philosophical outlook that we can
respect, one that is challenging to our own philosophical con-
victions.

One such worthy antagonist, and in my opinion the most
sensitive, the most intelligent and therefore the most penetrating,
was the Spanish philosopher José Ortega y Gasset, who was born
in Madrid in 1883 and died there in 1955. Ortega was by no
means a reactionary figure: in many spheres of thought, in
sociology and political science, in history and education, in
literary criticism and biography, as well as in ethics and metaphysics, he was one of the most eloquent and most intelligent men
of our time. If he had written in English or French or German,
his name would now be familiar to everyone. But he wrote in
Spanish, a language that makes its way slowly in the world; and
in addition he was deliberately informal, which does not please
the academic critic nor even the commercial publisher. Ortega
always refused to confine his vital thoughts within the rigid
framework of a system; from the first to the last of his writings,
he remained open to the diversity and complexity – one might

even say the intrinsic ambiguity – of experience. This does not mean, of course, that he ever refused to take up a position of his own, or even, if the occasion demanded, that he did not display a prejudice. In general one might even say that the position he took up was an extreme one – it was fixed at a geographical point, the Mediterranean. He would have been quick to claim that there is nothing extreme about such a point, which, as the word indicates, is in the middle of the world, but one could have retorted that it was his own Spanish people who were chiefly responsible for disturbing the equilibrium of the Ancient World by their discovery and conquest of a New World. But even before the discovery of America that equilibrium had been upset by invasions from and excursions to the East and the North, and it is significant that Ortega himself had to go to Germany to secure a grounding in philosophy.

Nevertheless, the Mediterranean remains useful as a cultural concept, and Ortega was to spend most of his mental energies vindicating it. Perhaps he had to go to the North to become aware of qualities in his own culture that might otherwise have been too conventional to deserve comment. As a Mediterranean man he had lived habitually with 'the harsh fierceness of the actual', one of his own expressions, and he had to discover that there was an alternative, namely, to retire into what a Northern poet has called the Interior Court, the world of impressions, intimations and essences. But he became aware of this alternative sphere of existence only to reject it – 'for a Mediterranean person,' he affirmed in his first book, 'the important thing is not the essence of an object, but its presence, its actuality'.[1] 'As long as we do not distinguish between things and the appearance of things,' he declared, 'what is most genuine in Southern art will escape our understanding.'

He tended to identify Northern art with impressionism, 'the will to find the sensuous as such', and he would not allow us Northerners to call ourselves realists. Only when the impression has been registered, measured, subjected to civilized order, that is to say, *thought*, does it become a real thing, capable of being used to build up our personality and our way of life. Vision, he said, 'becomes complete only through the concept. Sensation gives us the impression of things, not the things themselves.'[2]

At the same time, Ortega was well aware of the danger of a conceptual approach to art, for that might lead to the dehumanization of art, the title of one of his later books. He got out of this difficulty by two ruses – one was to point to the occasional nature of the concept, in itself a ruse to make philosophy possible. The Greeks, in his opinion, had invented the concept not exactly as an instrument of thought, but rather as one of observation. In other words, concepts are formed in order to give meaning to our observations; far from being a substitute for the spontaneity of life, conceptualization (according to Ortega) is actually the process by means of which we make life intelligible and secure. In Ortega's own words, 'the concept is clarity within life, the light shed on things, nothing more, nothing less'.[3] This word 'clarity' was to remain the key-word in all Ortega's thought, and it is an ideal to which we must give our most sympathetic attention, without, however, being intimidated by its emotive force.

The second ruse employed by Ortega takes the form of a paradox – the ideal, which again is present in his philosophy from its beginnings, of a *vital reason*. This, to me personally, is a most seductive ideal and closely corresponds to that synthesis of reason and romanticism which was my own first essay in philosophical criticism, written long before I had become acquainted with Ortega's work. The idea was not in either case an original one – it had been taking shape ever since the time of the early romantic philosophers, Schelling and Novalis, and is present already in Goethe's poetry. It gained a new dimension, a biological dimension, in the philosophy of Bergson, and Bergson had influenced Ortega. The basis for this idea is the evident fact that life itself, as a force and as a principle, is difficult to apprehend in its essential nature, which is its *living* nature. 'We murder to dissect', as Wordsworth said; or, in Bergson's terms, intelligence can seize only the discontinuous, life deprived of movement, death. Spain's other outstanding contemporary philosopher, Unamuno, had been stressing the same fact all his life: reason, he said, is the enemy of life; the mind seeks the dead because the living escapes it.

Ortega could not accept this dichotomy of life and reason, and his main effort as a philosopher was directed to the formation of a convincing synthesis of these polarities. He relied mainly on a logical analysis of the two concepts, though he was careful to point out that logic was no longer the inflexible instrument of analysis that had been handed down from classical times: alternative logics are nowadays available and knowledge itself is only one form of the rich morphology of thinking.[4] My own supposition, and admittedly it is not based on an altogether complete knowledge of Ortega's work, is that he had been impressed by the biological foundations of Bergson's philosophy and although he could not accept Bergson's criticism of the intellect, nevertheless he realized that life itself was the reality, and reason merely a form and function of that reality. He may at this point have been influenced by Nietzsche; there is an element in his thought which his disciple Mora has called *perspectivism*, perhaps derived from Schopenhauer and other Germanic concepts of the *will*: for example, he uses the phrase 'a will to concreteness'.[5]

I am not objecting to this teleological type of humanism – on the contrary, it is the only kind of humanism that is grounded in the biological facts. My own tendency, however, in so far as I have pursued it, is to rely on more recent psychological investigations, which are, in their turn, also biological facts – to trace these facts to their genetic origins, as notably Piaget has done. For then, in tracing the origins not only of intelligence, but of all the faculties that distinguish the human mind, we discover how intimately the vital organism, in its first groping contact with an indifferent material environment, rises from sensation and feeling to concepts and intelligence. Reason does indeed emerge as a form and function of life, but not as a separate organ – 'an organ', as Ortega would have it, 'or apparatus for the possession of things . . . an organ by means of which we capture things'.[6]

The only organ involved in that enterprise is perception, which is something more than mere sensation. Ortega says truly that sensation gives us the impression of things, not the things themselves. But as the Gestalt psychologists have so clearly demonstrated, there is already in the act of perception a sense of equilibrium or balance, a rudimentary pleasure principle, and what determines the completeness of vision is not the concept, but the percept. This is the basis of any criticism I have to offer of Ortega's rich and illuminating philosophy: it remains too intellectual in its premises. 'Only when something has been *thought*,' says Ortega, 'does it come within our power.' 'Only when a connection has been *seen and felt*,' I would say, 'does something come within our power.' And this, I would suggest, is the only sense in which reason can be said to be a form and function of life. In the rich morphology of thinking, the thinking eye, as Paul Klee called it, is perhaps the most vital form of reason. It is not sufficient for the eye to see: it must see the object against its background, in relation to other objects: see and connect.

It would seem at times that this is precisely what Ortega himself believed: 'I am myself and my circumstances' is one of his famous sayings. But Ortega's aim is to conceive of himself in relation to his circumstances, to realize himself as an intelligence at the centre of a visible array of harsh facts, an intelligence capable of separating and defining the multiplicity of sensations, discovering among them a hierarchy of values. Hence his ideal of clarity, the Mediterranean ideal *par excellence* according to Ortega.[7] The mind engages the chaos of sensations with this vital function: simply to make sense of one's circumstances, and life only gains significance in so far as the mind, that is to say, reason, exercizes this vital function.

And so we arrive at the typical Mediterranean ideal of *clarity*, a word that punctuates all Ortega's writings.

It is, of course, an attractive ideal, and has had a great appeal to the intelligence of men everywhere, perhaps especially in the dark and gloomy North. One thinks of Goethe's enthusiasm for this classical ideal – Shelley's too. But it is not the only possible ideal, and, indeed, there does exist an antithetical ideal, even on the level of sensation – not an ideal of darkness, much less of dinginess, which is perhaps the true antithesis of clarity. But an ideal of the nuance, of subtle shades and indefinite outlines: the *Autumn* of Keats.

Season of mists and mellow fruitfulness – the numerous celebrations, in English poetry and English painting, of twilight and night, even of darkness itself as the source of inspiration and vision. 'Tender is the night.' The nightingale, that sings in darkness, is an immortal bird, endlessly celebrated, ever consoling,

> Darkling I listen . . .
> Now more than ever seems it rich to die,
> To cease upon the midnight with no pain

Perhaps Byron best expresses this ideal of essential Night:

> All Heaven and earth are still – though not in sleep,
> But breathless, as we grow when feeling most;
> And silent, as we stand in thoughts too deep: –
> All heaven and earth are still: From the high host
> Of stars, to the lull'd lake and mountain-coast,
> All is concentrated in a life intense,
> Where not a beam, nor air, nor leaf is lost,
> But hath a part of being, and a sense
> Of that which is of all Creator and defence.
> Then stirs the feeling infinite . . .
> A truth, which through our being then doth melt
> And purifies from self: it is a tone,
> The soul and source of music, which make known
> Eternal harmony . . .
>   . . . Oh night,
> And storm, and darkness, ye are wondrous strong,
> Yet lovely in your strength . . .
>   . . . Most glorious night!
> Thou wert not sent for slumber! Let me be
> A sharer in thy fierce and far delight, –
> A portion of the tempest and of thee!

One could quote these tributes to Darkness and Night endlessly, they are so dear to the romantic spirit of the North, a spirit that spread across the Atlantic, to Whitman and Emily Dickinson, to Longfellow whose best poem is a *Hymn to Night:*

> From the cool cisterns of the midnight air
>   My spirit drank repose;
> The fountain of perpetual peace flows there, –
> From those deep cisterns flows . . .

The philosophical equivalent of such a love of darkness is an affirmation of the positive nature of doubt and indeterminacy – now, if we understand modern physicists correctly, even a scientific principle or hypothesis. It is true that Ortega himself realized that doubt is not something opposed to belief, but rather itself 'a kind of belief';[8] and he was sufficiently aware of this philosophical distinction to avoid dogmatic attitudes in his own thought. But this concession in philosophy did not involve any dimming of the ideal of clarity when it was a question of culture. That, being a question of environment or circumstance, was a question of 'pure nerve and pure muscle', a question of rescuing life from the abyss of insecurity.[9] Culture is precisely that: the moment of security, of certainty, of clarity in the midst of the environing chaos.[10] 'All cultural endeavour,' Ortega writes in his *Meditations on Quixote,* 'is an interpretation – elucidation, explanation or exegesis of life. Life is the eternal text. . . . Culture – art, science or politics – is the commentary, it is that aspect of life in which, by an act of self-reflection, life acquires polish and order. That is why the work of culture can never retain the problematic character pertaining to all that is merely living. In order to master the unruly torrent of life the learned man meditates, the poet quivers, and the political hero erects the fortress of his will. It would be odd indeed if the result of all these efforts led only to duplicating the problem of the universe. No, man has a mission of clarity upon earth.'[11]

To this ideal are opposed all forms of impressionism – perhaps Ortega would have said, the whole Romantic Tradition, which is surely indicated in this declaration, which comes from his *Meditations on Quixote:* 'An artistic style which does not contain the key to its own interpretation, which consists of a mere reaction of one part of life – the individual heart – to the rest of it, will produce only ambiguous values.'[12]

Before we return to Ortega's specific reflections on modern art, let us see what there is to be said for ambiguity in art, with the whole range of Western Art in mind, but more particularly the art of the Middle Ages, which best represents this ideal opposed to Mediterranean clarity.[13]

First we must observe that the distinction between these two ideals (of clarity and impressionism) is not a question of their *relative* humanism. Humanism is just as vague a category as romanticism, and the claim of the partisans of any particular age, such as the Age of Enlightenment (the seventeenth and eighteenth centuries) to be more humanistic than another age is preposterous, unless we are to deny the humanity of all spiritual values. It is true that man has from time to time asserted his self-sufficiency, his faith in himself, his independence of divine inspiration, and humanism in that sense is 'all too human'. The point I wish to make is that belief is not less essentially human than unbelief, or metaphysics less essentially human than physics. Romanesque and Gothic art are not less essentially human than the art of the Renaissance. What changes, in all this phantasmagoria of the human mind, is not humanity but its mode of representation.

No one was perhaps more aware of this relativism of all human thought than Ortega, but it is doubtful whether he would have conceded to the humanism of the Middle Ages, for example, the actuality or philosophical value that he found in the humanism of the Hellenistic world. And yet, seen without prejudice, the humanism of the Middle Ages is far more comprehensive than classical humanism, and precisely because it encompasses the dark as well as the rational. 'This humanism of the Middle Ages,' observes one of its greatest historians, Henri Focillon, 'as it emerges from the study of the monuments, clearly goes very far beyond any definition which might seek to limit it to a more or less precarious heritage from classical antiquity. There is, of course, a humanism of the humanists, but there is also another, wider in scope, and, one may perhaps say, more sincere, since it owes little to tradition and much more to life itself. The grandeur of its vision of man and of his relationship with the universe is revealed to us in medieval art. It does not present man in isolation. It shows him at grips with the exigencies, the miseries and the splendours of his destiny. It does not dwell on the bloom of his youth – save when it lays him at last upon his tomb – but shows him at every age, in every condition, toiling, and enduring. The blind man high on Rheims Cathedral proclaims the twin glories of divine justice and human patience. To the sweetness of the Gospels, to the majesty of theology, the humanism of the images adds the strength of its sympathy for all things living, a wonderful compassion and sincerity and openness of heart. It encompasses all things and sets man in the centre, and this image of God is all humanity. In this context the word humanity attains its full meaning. The superb humanity of Greek sculpture is incomplete. It exists in the sphere of the incorruptible, and is so categorical an affirmation of man that it dedicates him to solitude. The Middle Ages, on the other hand, immerse him on every side in the stream of things animate and inanimate. . . .'[14]

This wonderful passage, which sees in the medieval cathedrals, 'not memorials of their own time only, but our completest and most coherent presentation of man and his ideas', would hardly have appealed to a Spaniard who could praise Velasquez and Goya, but in El Greco could see only 'something of a regression'.[15] And yet this period of darkness and confusion had established, long before the Renaissance, the very principle that was to be so dear to Ortega, the substantiality of light, which had been identified with the divine source of life, with the Godhead, by St Augustine and translated into a lantern of radiant stone by the Abbot Suger at Saint-Denis (*Plate 44*), right at the beginning of the Gothic period.[16]

These observations are in no sense fractious, but I approach my main purpose, which is to examine Ortega's concept of humanism in relation to modern art. Ortega, as the title of his most relevant essay indicates, saw in the whole development of modern art a process of dehumanization, and his thesis stands or falls on the validity of his concept of humanism. This essay was written before 1925, the date of the first edition of the volume in which it appeared. We must remember this date if we are to criticize Ortega, for the process which he observed at that time has now reached an extreme that he could hardly have foreseen, though this kind of extremism is exactly what he had in mind in a later essay 'On Extremism as a Form of Life,' which was included in a posthumous volume which appeared in 1956, a year after Ortega's death.[17] But in 1925 the seeds of these later developments of art were already evident to a perceptive critic like Ortega: Cubism, Futurism, Dadaism and Surrealism, and various forms of abstract art had already proliferated their main features, and it may be doubted if forty years later the manifestations of contemporary art contain anything essentially new.

Ortega suggested in *The Dehumanization of Art* that modern art would always be unpopular because it is extreme: it is essentially unpopular, he said, moreover, it is antipopular. The more recent proliferation of popular publications on modern art, the immense crowds that have been attracted to certain exhibitions of modern art in the larger cities throughout the world, and the appearance of a late phase of modern art that is actually called popular ('pop-art'), might seem to throw some doubt on Ortega's assertion, but I am willing to concede his point for, crowds or no crowds, the masses do not *understand* modern art. It is an art for the minority, an esoteric art, and remains most esoteric when it would be most popular. On account of that fact Ortega proceeds to his main deduction, which is, that not being accessible to every man, the impulses of this art are not of 'a generically human kind' – which, incidentally, is the charge that Tolstoy brought against modern art. A further echo of Tolstoy is evident when Ortega proceeds to answer his own rhetorical question: what happens in the minds of people when they 'like' a work of art? The answer is easy, he says: A man likes a play, for example, when he has become interested in the human destinies presented to him, 'when the love and hatred, the joys and sorrows of the personages so move his heart that he participates in it all as though it were happening in real life. . . . In poetry he seeks the passion and the pain of the man behind the poet. Paintings attract him if he finds on them figures of men and women whom it would be interesting to meet.'[18] And so on: for most people, art as they understand it is a means through which they are brought in contact with interesting human affairs.

This is the doctrine of socialist realism, still current in orthodox communist countries. But Ortega does not, of course, support such a naïve doctrine. He proceeds to point out that 'preoccupation with the human content of the work is in principle incompatible with aesthetic enjoyment proper'. Indeed, 'an object of art is artistic only in so far as it is not real'.[19] We are forced to the conclusion, therefore, that there are two kinds of art, one for the minorities and one for the majority, and Ortega points out that it is only the latter kind that has always been realistic. He gives as an example the Middle Ages, when there existed an aristocratic art that was 'conventional' and 'idealistic', and a popular art that was realistic and satirical. He might have given other examples – the hieratic and the popular arts of Ancient Egypt or of China. Such a division is, indeed, a universal tendency within the history of art.

This dichotomy, according to Ortega, can be stretched in the conventional or idealistic type of art to a point at which the human content has grown so thin that it is negligible, and that is the point we have reached today. He lists seven characteristics of modern art which he thinks prove his contention:

Modern art is (1) dehumanized; (2) it avoids living forms; (3) it is nothing but a work of art; (4) it is play and nothing else; (5) it is essentially ironical; (6) it aspires to scrupulous realization; and (7) art ends by becoming a thing of no consequence.

Of these seven features of modern art, it is the tendency to dehumanization which Ortega regards as most characteristic, and indeed the other features may be said to be a consequence of this one tendency. But what does Ortega mean by dehumanization and to what extent does he condemn this tendency? He admits that the tendency is inevitable, that it is from another point of view the essential element of *style* in art. His charge is limited to the fact that in his opinion this tendency has been carried too far: 'stylization has strangled the living subject. With the objects of modern pictures no intercourse is possible. By divesting them of their aspect of "lived" reality the artist has blown up the bridges and burned the ships that could have taken us back to our daily world. He leaves us locked up in an abstruse universe with which human dealings are inconceivable. . . . This new way of life which presupposes the annulment of spontaneous life is precisely what we call understanding and enjoyment of art.'[20]

It should by now be obvious that what Ortega objects to in modern art is its tendency to abstraction. Though he argues that a purely abstract art is not feasible, for 'even in the most abstract ornamental line a stubborn reminiscence lurks of certain "natural" forms', nevertheless, the intention of the modern artist is an explicit act of dehumanization.

At times it would seem that Ortega wants the best of two inconsistent worlds: he realizes that 'style involves dehumanization', that style is 'the royal road of art'; and yet to be human in the fullest sense of the term means to follow reality, to abandon style. And so we arrive at the typical Mediterranean compromise, the Greek – or perhaps one should say the Aristotelian – doctrine of the mean, of measure, the high noon of the intellect.

Ortega was far too intelligent a philosopher to dismiss the extremism of modern art as an aberration of the mind, a twilight of the intellect. He realized that it is an historical phenomenon that has grown from a multitude of entangled roots, but he thought that an explanatory investigation of the kind required was too serious a task for him to attempt. He concluded his polemic with a final all-embracing charge: the modern movement is a disguised attack on art itself – 'a mask which conceals surfeit with art and hatred of it'; and he hinted that this was but one aspect of a wider phenomenon, the rankling grudge which modern Western man bears against his own historical essence.

That modern art in its essence is closely bound to the social and economic developments of our time is a truth that we must all admit: it shares those elements of revolts and dissolution, of violence and fragmentation, of destruction and reconstruction, that give the political development of Europe in our time its intrinsic ambiguity. But that does not make art less 'human'; on the contrary, it gives to art its relevance, its significance, its intrinsic honesty. Even if we consider the aspect of modern art that most shocked Ortega, its will to abstraction, which he was willing to dismiss as a perverse kind of modesty on the artist's part, a refusal to be involved in the vulgarities of the modern age, even here we must protest that at its best, in the architecture of Mies van der Rohe, in the paintings of Mondrian or the sculpture of Gabo, such an art is by no means a negative art, an art without pretences. On the contrary, such art has the highest and most positive purpose, the will to create a new reality: to escape from the confusion and arbitrariness of the historical present and to visualize the paradigms, the prototypes of a new and a better civilization. If it is a question of full clarity, of the high noon of the intellect, I do not know where such qualities are to be found if not in the work of these modern artists.

But I must not leave the reader with the impression that modern art is redeemed by a few idealists like Mies van der Rohe or Gabo. My whole contention is that the life of the intellect is only one half of life, and that corresponding to this hemisphere of light is the hemisphere of darkness, equally insistent on recognition, on representation. I speak in metaphors, but what I am hypostatizing is the concurrent existence of two worlds, the world of Intellect and the world of Instinct; and the whole purpose and proof of modern psychology has been to insist on the right and indeed, for individual and social health, the necessity of coming to terms with the dark side of our human cosmos. 'Freud found intellect only a hope,' writes one of the best of his commentators, 'a hope, not a description, and the essential and fundamental thing Instinct. Thought was a derived or secondary phenomenon, like neuroses an inevitable accident of frustrated Instinct.'[21] Freud eclipses the high noon of the intellect with his theory of the libido, but contrary to the opinion of some of his interpreters, he does offer us some hope, and it is precisely through art. His interpretation of art as an overcoming of neurosis or mental sickness is too narrow, but at least it does explain the significance of that type of art which Ortega despises – or at least fails to understand: the art that corresponds to the dark night of the soul rather than to the high noon of the intellect.

It is with a sense of betrayal that I take leave of Ortega on this critical note. Ortega was not a reactionary philosopher; on the contrary, he welcomed the fact that modern man orients himself in the future, and not – like the man of the Middle Ages and indeed the man of the Ancient World – in the past.[22] He gives what is perhaps the best expression to this open attitude in that brilliant essay which he wrote in 1932 for the centenary of Goethe's death. Protesting against Goethe's passivism, his 'bloodless Wertherism', his refusal to live his destiny, he cries: 'Living is precisely the inexorable necessity to make oneself determinate, to *enter into an exclusive destiny*, to accept it – that is, to resolve to *be it*. We *have*, whether we like it or not, to realize our "personage," our vocation, our vital program, our "entelechy"– there is no lack of names for the terrible reality which is our authentic I (ego).'[23] That is precisely the belief of the best of our modern artists, and their extremism is but one other name for the terrible reality which is our authentic ego.

IX

The Disintegration of Form in Modern Art

Before I speak of the disintegration of form in modern art, I should perhaps define what I mean by art's integrity.

Art is a biological phenomenon: that is my basic assumption. Art has been present as a characteristic of the human race ever since the species emerged from the obscurity of prehistory, and there is plenty of evidence to suggest that art, which is the skill required to give meaningful shape to human artifacts, was one of the agencies of that emergence. Man became civilized to the degree that he could refine on mere utility, on the tools and husbandry that had been essential to survival. Even the social aspects of the earliest civilizations can be called 'civil' only to the degree that they rise above expediency to effect principles of equity or justice – principles that imply a sensitive discrimination in human relations. As Plato argued in his *Politicus*, the state is also, or should be, a work of art.

The immediate purpose of the creative effort that goes to the making of a work of art was the refinement of man's powers of perception and discrimination, and this purpose was achieved by an ever-progressive apprehension of the subtleties of form. Whether we look at the process ontogenetically or phylogenetically, we see the human organism acquiring command of its

Originally given as a lecture on September 28, 1964, in connection with *Documenta III* Exhibition at Kassel, Germany.

environment by an increasing ability to discriminate between one form and another, and this power of discrimination is *aesthetic* – that is to say, a power based on the education and training of the senses – the senses of sight, touch and hearing. To discriminate between the comparative significance of a form, or the significance of that form in the field of total sensation – such is the aesthetic faculty and it is the faculty that gradually differentiated man from the rest of the animal kingdom, gave him that self-consciousness which is the basis of his religion and his science, and led to the ever increasing fertility of his mind and imagination. It follows that any moment in history that leads to a dulling of the sensibilities, to a relaxation of the consciousness of form, is a retrograde movement, leading to the decline of human civilization. And that, I believe, is the present threat to our civilization.

I have so far used the word *form* to distinguish the object of a discriminating consciousness, but in one place I spoke of the *subtleties* of form, and in this manner I began to introduce an important qualification. Form is an impersonal concept – a theoretical or absolute concept – and what exist in our human situation are various approximations to ideal forms. I do not intend to be metaphysical at this point: all I mean is that between a perfect circle as drawn by a compass and our immediate apprehension and representation of a circle is a difference determined by our individual organs of sensibility. In perception and execution we approximate to mathematical laws, and as all sensitive philosophers of art have observed, what we call a work of art preserves these approximations. Sometimes we call it 'the human touch'. Ruskin expressed the same truth when he said that all genuine works of art were the result of mathematical laws 'organically transgressed'. The point is that what we call life and what we call law are basically incompatible: life exceeds the law, for the sake of adventure, of advance, perhaps merely for the sake of a necessary freedom, a freedom to play. In other words, there are in every genuine work of art (and by 'genuine' we mean something that serves a biological purpose, something that is *genetically* advantageous) two elements, one of a mathematical nature which gives rise to the category of *beauty* and one of an organic nature which gives rise to the category of *vitality*. The greatest works of art are those that combine these two elements in a form which we call organic because it possesses both beauty and vitality.

If the formal elements in a work of art are in their essence absolute and immutable, those elements that make it organic are by contrast flexible and entative, advancing by trial and error, achieving effectiveness by individual effort. This power in an individual to achieve the effectiveness of any organic activity we call *style*, and it is as essential to art's integrity as is form. Form becomes organic by virtue of an individual's ability to refine form until it has vitality. This is always a personal achievement – that is to say, there is nothing concrete or measurable about the quality thus achieved: it is a presence, *une durée pure* in Bergson's sense, and cannot be apprehended by the intellect. It is accessible only to that faculty we call intuition, and no amount of scientific scepticism has been able to deprive us of this necessary word to indicate powers or processes so far inaccessible to scientific observation. There is always in a work of art this intangible, indefinable element to which it owes its vitality, its magical power to enhance life, and an artist's possession of this transforming power is his style.

All great periods of art are vital in this sense and all individual works of art in such periods possess style. It is only in decadent and academic periods that the vitality of art is sacrificed to rules and formulas; only in such periods that individuality and eccentricity are despised. The modern movement in art has been an immense effort, that has now lasted for more than a century, to restore to art its vital function, to make art once more an organic mode of perception and communication. Delacroix, Courbet, Constable, Turner, Degas, Cézanne, Matisse, Picasso, Gabo, Moore – these are some of the representative artists who gradually redeemed art from its academic sterility and made it once more an expression of man's expanding apprehension of reality.

Such is art's integrity: an unrelenting concentration on formal unity, on stylistic vitality, to the end that art serves the evolving consciousness of mankind in the total effort to establish a human world in the midst of an indifferent universe.

Let us now contemplate the forces that threaten art's integrity: the modes of disintegration which I shall review under the categories of *incoherence*, *insensitivity*, *brutality* and *privacy*.

The whole of the modern movement is sometimes accused of incoherence, but such criticism generally confuses incoherence with a very different quality, informality (cf. Chapter IV). Incoherence is the failure to reach, or a deliberate disregard of, integrity of form; incoherence is chaos.

Informality, by which we generally mean *irregularity* of form, is not necessarily chaotic. Nature is full of organic forms that are superficially irregular. It may be that every form in nature – and there is no reason why we should confine our observations to organic forms – can be explained as the result of an interaction of forces, electro-magnetic or cosmic – that are measurable or predictable, but to the human eye, aided or not by the microscope, many of the structures of matter have an informal character. Such structures appeal to our aesthetic sensibility for reasons which we cannot explain – they fascinate us. Obvious examples are cumulus clouds in a clear sky; stains on walls; patterns of lichen on trees; irregular rock formations, especially those eroded by wind or sea-water. But there are a myriad of such irregular forms in nature which for some mysterious reason have this same kind of fascination.

The modern artist can create forms that are irregular in this sense and of similar attractiveness. The movement known as Abstract Expressionism is devoted to the exploration of this realm of irregular form, and there is no doubt that the individual artist can endow such forms with style and vitality. Their deeper significance is not to be excluded: they may be archetypal forms, corresponding to some psychic syndrome in the artist's mind. If that syndrome is personal, it may elicit in the spectator nothing more than curiosity or sympathy, hardly aesthetic feelings. But the archetypal shapes may be of universal significance if we can accept Jung's hypothesis of a collective unconscious. It is difficult to explain the extremes of informality (for example some of the paintings of American artists such as De Kooning, Sam Francis, Jackson Pollock, Franz Kline, etc. (*Plates 55–57, 59*) on any other supposition. Even if they record no more than the graph of a gesture, the gesture, in so far as it is not aimless and therefore incoherent, is presumably significant: the calligraph records a state of mind.

Incoherence is meaningless: it is the disruption of all significant relationships, and corresponds to the débris left by an earthquake. There are contemporary artists who do not hesitate to expose the débris of a mental disturbance that corresponds to an earthquake. Such a formal distintegration is usually accompanied by another threat to art's integrity: lack of style, or insensitivity.

Style, as Goethe once observed, belongs to the deepest foundations of personality. It is a visible record of the encounter that takes place in the psyche between spirit and matter, and it tells us to what extent, in this arena, spirit has been able to shape matter to meet its own need for externalization or expression. As individuals thrown into society we are compelled to communicate with one another, not merely for mutual aid in the struggle for survival, but for self-assurance, indeed, for self-awareness. We become individuals only to the extent that we declare our differences, and we declare our differences by objectifying them in gestures of various kinds. At a primitive level such gestures may be merely a tone of voice, a facial expression, an habitual posture or movement. But if we wish to stabilize such expressions of individuality we create an object that bears their impress. Some works of art are no more than this: expressions of the self, but we must always, as T. S. Eliot once told us, have a self to express. More often, however, we do not create objects whose sole purpose is to represent a self: instead we represent the self in all we make, so that whether we are painting a picture or building a house or making a chair, we leave some trace of our uniqueness on what we make. That trace of our uniqueness is our style, and though we may be influenced by the manner in which other individuals have expressed or are expressing their uniqueness, we are judged to have a good style if we are true to our own self, our unique sensibility.

It is sometimes said that we can express the self merely by the selection we make of available images – that the quest for originality is a vain one and in any case a waste of effort. This is one of the excuses used to justify 'pop-art', or any kind of self-expression that dispenses with style. Such non-art has been called 'the art that looks sideways', which seems to be a confession of its evasiveness. We may agree that the label 'pop-art' is misleading; that 'the art in it is far from pop' and that 'the pop is there precisely because it is anti-art'. What is meant by an art that is anti-art is really an art that is completely lacking in style, and it is this personal factor that certain artists now wish to sacrifice, without, however, sacrificing the art market. Objects must still be made because there is no traffic in subjective states of mind.

There is, we are told in this same context, 'a nostalgic admiration for the images that are undeniably common objects. Nothing is lower than a pictorial bubble-gum wrapper, yet it possesses, effortlessly and automatically, of its nature, the property that is most desired for art. The nostalgia mingles with another longing, the longing for material that will be genuinely un-acceptable and stick in the cultivated gullet as real art should. These requirements, however sophisticated they may sound, are real needs. There is a desperation in them and it has swept aside some of the most cherished assumptions of modern painting.'[1]

We can understand the desire to create an art that sticks in the cultivated gullet 'as real art should' – that has been the desire of all artists in revolt against the academic traditions of the past. That was certainly the desire of the Dadaists and the Surrealists in our time, and one of the most boring aspects of the art mis-leadingly called pop-art is its repetition of gestures that stuck in the cultivated gullet fifty years ago but that were long ago swallowed and discarded because they had served their purpose. There is nothing new in pop-art, least of all its use of popular images taken from cigarette packets and comic strips; exactly the same kind of débris was exploited by artists like Kurt Schwitters, Picabia, Marcel Duchamp and Man Ray. But there is this difference: in their extreme revolt against cultivated art the Dadaists remained artists – that is to say, they retained their style. Even when, as in the case of Marcel Duchamp, no style was involved, but rather the selection and isolation of 'a certain kind of object', the gesture was as ephemeral as it was witty. It was not intended as a joke to be repeated.

It may be said that even a joke may have style, and that is true. Every human gesture, so long as it is expressive, has style, which is the justification of action painting. But the gesture must have some emphatic purpose, it must send the ball into that part of the tennis court where we least expect it, where it wins a point. A monotonous gesture has no style: it is the epitome of boredom.

An absence of style leads to the apotheosis of brutality. That this quality should be offered as a substitute for style is perhaps not surprising in an age distinguished for its vandalism and criminal violence. It is probably motivated and to some extent justified as a revolt against sophistication and refinement, and it is significant that it is more prevalent in architecture than in the other arts (though it has analogues in literature). In architecture it has some obvious advantages: it saves money and therefore appeals to the insensitive business man. Its visual aspect is clumsiness, and a brutal gesture in art is just as ugly as a brutal gesture in behaviour.

A brutal gesture may be used to inspire terror, and there are legitimate effects in art when terror, or *terribilità*, is the means. Beauty and terror, for some mysterious reason, lie very close together, but where we find them associated in a work of art, the significant fact is their association, not the presence of one or the other element. Terror is introduced, in a Greek or Elizabethan drama, to produce catharsis, to leave a stillness that seems all the more intense after the passage of the storm. But this is not the aim of our contemporary brutalists, who are not able to effect a synthesis of terror and beauty, but leave their public in a state of displeasure and distress.

What I have with some hesitation called *privacy* is a very ubiquitous characteristic of modern art and one which deserves more consideration than it has hitherto been given. We speak of a private joke, meaning a joke that cannot be generally understood or appreciated, a joke that is perhaps only funny to the joker. More and more of our younger artists perpetrate jokes of this kind in their paintings and sculpture. The anonymous author of the statement I have already quoted suggests that 'the idea of *expression* and the idea of the artist as someone in communication with us through some code that we can decipher are inadequate to the situation. The idea of the relationship between artist and spectator as in any way analogous to a verbal relationship is totally obsolete, and obsolete not only for Albers and Kline but equally for Appel and Giacometti. All that we know is that the maker of art felt the need of a certain kind of object in his life – in his studio – and proceeded to make it. And that others, seeing the object, recognize the need and find it satisfied.'

This seems to be a very illogical situation. The artist, we are told, has no desire to communicate with us: he just makes 'a certain kind of object' which he needs to have around, to satisfy a private need. But if we invade his privacy, then he may find that after all his private object satisfies our private need. In other words, he has made a communication, he has expressed himself in a sign or symbol that has general significance.

That seems to be an uncommon piece of luck, and if the intruder into his privacy happens to be a collector or a dealer who also has a need for 'a certain kind of object', then the indifferent artist is luckier still – his private needs have become public investments. But is that always the situation? Is it not more likely that the artist, or 'the maker of art' as he is now called, 'feeling the need' makes an object that has no significance for anyone but himself, an object without beauty or vitality, an object of non-art?

Such is, indeed, what happens in the majority of cases. These brutal scribbles and scrawls, these assemblages of rusty junk from the scrap-heap or dump, what meaning or significance can they have for 'others' unless some concession is made to the idea of a relationship between artist and spectator? Art *is* communication, and though every method and every kind of material is legitimate, materials and methods must establish a visual relationship between the artist and the spectator. Art always was and must remain a mode of symbolic discourse, and where there is no symbol and therefore no discourse, there is no art. Not to affirm this, with all possible conviction, is to betray a sacred trust.

I ought to be more specific, to name the artists and critics who have betrayed this trust. I hesitate to do this, not only because their name is legion, but also because the movement disowns the very concept of personal responsibility. The whole purpose of art as a creative and cognitive activity is called in question. What we are witnessing is not merely the disintegration of form in art, but the disintegration of intelligence itself, a descent into the eternal 'fun fair' which is neither funny nor fair, but an inferno into which the intellectually alienated and morally insensitive vandals of an urban economy descend in their ruthless search for any object on which to expend their destructive energies.

Disintegration, by definition, has no unifying principle, but a label must be found to cover the diverse phenomena of the contemporary scene and so the term 'pop-art' came into vogue. It was coined on the analogy of pop-music, but pop-music is genuinely popular, a modern version of folk-music. It may be sophisticated, and it may contradict all the canons of academic music, but it springs from the people and serves their needs for stimulation and emotional release. Pop-art can make no such claim: it has no roots in mass-culture, and its claim to select and emphasize popular images is a delusion. What it exploits for the most part is a very different thing: the commercial image – that is to say, an image devised by cunning publicity agents to persuade the public to buy mass-produced goods (beverages, processed foods, cosmetics, gadgets of every kind) or, alternatively, persuade the same public to patronize some kind of entertainment (sport, cinema, dancing). Rather different, but still commercially motivated, are the various types of strip-cartoons which do certainly exploit the emotions of the masses, but do so not for any emotional satisfaction, but merely to promote the sale of a periodical carrying commercial advertisements. The whole range of such popular images is a by-product of competitive capitalism and as such does not exist in non-capitalist countries.

I do not make such an observation with an ethical bias: art has always been indifferent to moral laws. It is conceivable that the visual images invented for the exploitation of the public could be the subject-matter of a genuine pictorial art, and the work of the American painter, Stuart Davis, often claimed as a precursor of 'pop-art', is an example of a genuine art of this kind. But in the paintings of Stuart Davis (*Plate 60*) the images submit to an aesthetic discipline: they are composed as carefully as the images in an academic painting – indeed Stuart Davis might be criticized for his academic use of popular images. Occasionally a pop-artist may use this material with an intellectual acuteness and compositional skill that give the spectator a momentary shock of pleasure – this would explain the appeal of painters like Larry Rivers, Kitaj (*Plate 61*), and Rauschenberg. Such painters have a recognizable 'hand-writing' and assemble their visual débris with sensitive feeling for colour and composition. It is doubtful, however, if these remnants of an aesthetic conscience are enough to rescue their works from final incoherence.

It will be said that such aesthetic criteria are beside the point: this is anti-art, not art, and aesthetics is a dirty word. The pop-artist is like those atheists who make a religion of their disbelief: he does not accept any standards of judgement. He does not address any audience and does not represent any point of view. He echoes Goethe's poem from which the nihilist Max Stirner took his slogan: he has staked everything on nothingness:

Ich hab' mein sach' auf nichts gestellt

A philosophy of nihilism, of extreme egoism, is permissible, but it must be expressed coherently if it is to be taken seriously. And for all his scorn of moral and aesthetic values, of academic standards and artistic categories, the pop-artist does want to be taken seriously – otherwise why does he exhibit his works to the public and ask them to pay serious prices for them?

Finally, as a very perceptive critic has suggested (Anita Brookner in *The Burlington Magazine*, June 1964), this absence of standards is ultimately boring. In her review of the Gulbenkian Exhibition in the Tate Gallery, from the catalogue of which I have already made some quotations, she observes that 'these pictures are not merely dull (or strange or exciting); they are simply not explicit'. By this she means that though they may be 'explicit as to effect', they remain 'inscrutable as to cause'. A Dada painting had a *raison d'être*: to mock the pretentiousness and solemnity of academic art; Surrealist painting claimed to be 'in the service of the revolution'. Even the Futurists, though they loudly proclaimed their independence of all accepted values, their contempt for museums and libraries, nevertheless proposed new ideals. 'The world's splendour has been enriched by a new beauty: the beauty of speed' they declared in their first Manifesto. They rejected the ideals of 'harmony' and 'good taste', but in their place they put ideals like 'universal dynamism' and 'physical transcendentalism', even 'sincerity' and 'purity'. Pop-art has no ideal because as a movement it believes only in an involvement with whatever presents itself in urban activities. Pop-artists have no interest in nature, but subsitute for nature the visual chaos of their environment. Their involvement with life is promiscuous, and although they have to conform to certain physical limitations in order to assemble an effective image, they clutch at any dead cat in the city sewer.

They succeed in embarrassing the critics, and that may be one of their aims. To give serious consideration to their antics is to fall into the trap they have laid for us. They compel us to be solemn about silly matters, to prick toy balloons with scalpels. It is not the artists who provoke the critic, but people who have no sense of aesthetic values. Such people, because they are bored and alienated, accept instead of the work of art (which always demands concentration and effort on the part of the

53. *Wassily Kandinsky. Painting with White Forms. 1913*

55. *Jackson Pollock. Painting. 1956*

54. *Karel Appel.*
Personage. 1961

56. *Willem de Kooning. Gotham News. 1955*

57. *Sam Francis.* *The Over Yellow*

58. *Antonio Tapies. Ocre Graphique. 1960*

59. *Franz Kline. Abstraction. 1955*

60. Stuart Davis.
Lucky Strike. 1921

61. R. B. Kitaj.
An Early Europe. 1964

spectator) a sensational stimulus as brief and banal as any side-show in an amusement park. It is the art dealer and the museum director who is perhaps most to be blamed, for he provides the exhibition space; unfortunately, however, he can say quite truly that he is only giving the public what it wants.

And so in the end we arrive at the social problem – not so much the question of the role of the artist in society or the proper use of leisure in an affluent society, but rather the general problem of the decadence of our civilization.

I began by asserting that art was a biological phenomenon, closely connected with the development of self-consciousness and intelligence. The relation of individual development to social development is close and intricate: one might say that man evolves as a species but that the decisive steps are taken by individuals. The biologist would, of course, elaborate and qualify such a vague generalization, but the only point I wish to make would not be disputed – namely, that other men are part of the environment in which the individual develops his con-sciousness of the world. We are part of one another and our victories over nature are obtained by mutual aid.

Art is at once an activity that refines the sensibilities and an activity that invents and perfects symbols of discourse – these two aspects of human life are inseparable: self-integration and inter-communication.

The whole process, involving gesture, speech, the invention of signs and alphabets, the metaphorical representation of experience (myth, history, poetry, plastic art) is infinitely com-plex, but always at the emergent point of evolution, the bright focus of animal attention and intention, is the discriminating sensibility – that is to say, the aesthetic faculty. To relax or forego this nervous concentration of energy is to give up not so much the struggle for existence, for that depends on cunning and brute strength, but the will to live abundantly, the erotic overflow of energy into realms of freedom and delight.

This fine distinction between existence and delight, between satisfaction and pleasure, is achieved by the aesthetic process – by the discrimination of forms and the sensuous apprehension of thinghood, of that being-in-itself which exceeds being-for-a-purpose. This is not a metaphysical distinction: it is a purely practical distinction in the evolution of humanity, and on the awareness of this distinction is founded the whole fabric of civilization: not only metaphysical thought, but also scientific invention and everything we venture to call progress, meaning the alleviation of our brutish destiny.

It may seem difficult to equate all the various manifestations of art with this achievement of a human civilization, and admittedly we are using art in a very wide sense, in the sense of a progressive discrimination or refinement of perception. But it is this wide sense that covers all the historical manifestations of art (from the prehistoric cave paintings to pop-art) and it is the critic's task and duty to decide which of these various manifestations is positive and which negative. Art is in the service of life, criticism is in the service of life; any other supposition is a betrayal of our human destiny.

To what extent are we critics responsible for the present nihilistic phase of art? Is it a logical consequence of all we have striven for in the past fifty years? Does the movement that began with Cézanne and his resolve to wrest the secret of being from the visible universe lead logically and inevitably to the present disintegration of the visual image? I would wear sackcloth and ashes if I thought so. On the contrary, the great enterprise that was initiated by Cézanne has often gone astray and some of its outriders have been lost in the desert. But the main line of advance has been clear and consistent. Whether as an extension of perceptual experience or as a realization of inner feeling, the main purpose of the modern artist has been to establish being. He has redeemed vision from its merely reproductive task, the obsession of the degenerate Renaissance tradition, and has dared to be creative, that is to say, to transcend the accepted level of existence. I speak in somewhat Heideggerian terms, but Heidegger is the only modern philosopher who has seen that art has this vital and predominant purpose, namely, that it is an act of violence that discloses being. Art is what most immediately brings being *to stand*, stabilizes it in something present, that is to say, in the work of art. Art for this reason must always be revolutionary, for we cannot remain inactive in our existential situation (inactivity in this sense is a living death). We continually struggle with appearance, and against the nothingness that is death. We are always threatened by spiritual and mental disintegration, the prelude to physical disintegration and death, and art is the effort to resist disintegration, 'to recapture oneself out of confusion in appearance'. We cannot do this by thought, by intellection of any kind. Being can be disclosed only in an object, and the moment of disclosure is our awareness of the *logos* incorporated in the work of art.[2]

This great enterprise has been betrayed by the permissive art of today, the art which 'abandons the philosophic guides'. This art without concentration, without relationship, this art which boasts of its inconsequence and incoherence, is not art at all, and though some of its practitioners are undoubtedly sensitive they are like delinquent children who destroy a beautiful object shamelessly because they are not loved, because they resent the world they did not make, a darkening world indeed – a world characterized, in Heidegger's words, by 'the flight of the gods, the destruction of the earth, the standardization of man, the pre-eminence of the mediocre'.[3]

I have spent too much time on the criticism of a phase of modern art that is admittedly ephemeral, and may have gone out of fashion before these words can have any effect. But the social conditions that determine the emergence of such a kind of anti-art are not ephemeral: they are with us in increasing and frightening intensity. Until we can halt these processes of destruction and standardization, of materialism and mass communication, art will always be subject to the threat of disintegration. The genuine arts of today are engaged in a heroic struggle against mediocrity and mass values, and if they lose, then art, in any meaningful sense, is dead. If art dies, then the spirit of man becomes impotent and the world relapses into barbarism.

Text References

PREFACE

1. (p. 7), *The Life of Forms in Art.* English trans. of *La Vie des formes,* Paris, 1936. New York (Wittenborn), 1948

I ORIGINALITY

1. (p. 12), R. Goldschmidt, *The Material Basis of Evolution*, London and New Haven (Yale Univ. Press), 1940

2. (p. 13), The Bollingen Series, vol. XXIX. New York (Pantheon Books), 1951. Another translation has been made by Shih-Hsiang Chen and published privately by the Anthoensen Press, Portland, Maine, in 1953. I quote the translation of the same passage:

Such moments when Mind and Matter hold perfect communion,
And wide vistas open to regions hitherto entirely barred,
Will come with irresistible force,
And go, their departure none can hinder.
Hiding, they vanish like a flash of light;
Manifest, they are like sounds arising in mid-air.

So acute is the mind in such instants of divine comprehension,
What chaos is there that it cannot marshal in miraculous order?
While winged thoughts, like quick breezes, soar from depths of the heart,
Eloquent words, like a gushing spring, flow between lips and teeth.

No flower, or plant, or animal is too prodigal of splendour,
To be recreated under the writer's pen,
Hence the most wondrous spectacle that ever whelmed the eye,
And notes of the loftiest music that rejoiced the ear.

3. (p. 13), I take the literal version of this couplet from Professor Hughes's commentary.

4. (p. 13), *Zen through the Art of Archery*, by Eugen Herrigel, London (Routledge & Kegan Paul), 1953

5. (p. 14), *On Modern Art*, trans. Paul Findlay, London (Faber), 1948

6. (p. 16), May I confess at once my dependence at this point on a philosopher who has devoted almost a lifetime to this very problem, Leone Vivante. In two works in particular, both of which have been translated into English – *Intelligence in Expression with an Essay on Originality of Thought and its Physiological Conditions* and *Notes on the Originality of Thought: The Concept of Internal Necessity: Poetic Thought and Constructive Thought*,[7] the whole subject is explored with a subtlety and profundity which I cannot hope to rival: I can only express an indebtedness now of forty years standing to my Italian colleague.

7. Both translated by Professor Brodrick-Bullock, the first published by C. W. Daniel & Co. (London, 1925), the second by John Lane (London, 1927)

8. (p. 17), This is a view of poetry (and indeed of originality) that has been taken up by certain German philosophers, notably Ernst Cassirer and Martin Heidegger. Cf. Cassirer, *Language and Myth*, trans. Susanne K. Langer, New York (Harper), 1946; Heidegger, *Existence and Being*, London (Vision Press), 1949 ('Hölderlin and the Essence of Poetry')

9. (p. 18), *Poetic Diction: A Study in Meaning*, London (Faber & Gwyer), 1928, pp. 134-6. The whole of the chapter, on 'The Making of Meaning' from which this quotation is taken, is relevant to my argument.

10. (p. 19), *Op. cit.*, pp. 137-8

11. (p. 20), Quoted by Derek Stanford, *Christopher Fry: an Appreciation*, London (Peter Nevill), 1951, p. 94

12. (p. 21), *Biog. Literaria*, I, 15

13. (p. 22), London (Faber & Gwyer), 1928

14. (p. 24), By Georges Duthuit, in *The Fauvist Painters*, New York (Wittenborn), 1950, p. 21

15. (p. 24), Vol. I, 'Museum without Walls'; Vol. II, 'The Creative Art', trans. Stuart Gilbert, New York (Bollingen Series) and London (Zwemmer), 1949

16. (p. 26), This is Jung's gloss on Schiller. See *Psychological Types*, Chap. II, 'Schiller and the Type Problem' (Eng. trans., 1938, p. 155)

17. (p. 28), The forms he invents correspond no doubt to some quality in his make-up. But from Lu Chi to Malraux, all the authorities I have quoted are agreed that originality is found at the technical or formal stage of art: it has nothing to do with ideas or values, with the artist's religion or philosophy, his morals or his social environment: but only with the manipulation of the concrete materials of his art.

18. (p. 29), Harvard University Press, 1947, p. 53

19. (p. 29), London (Dennis Dobson), 1950

20. (p. 30), pp. 90-1. And cf. Victor Zuckerkandl, *Sound and Symbol*, New York (Bollingen Series) and London (Routledge & Kegan Paul), 1956, p. 222: 'It is not that the mind of the creative artist expresses itself in tones, words, colours, and forms as its medium; on the contrary, tone, word, colour, form express themselves through the medium of the creative mind.'

21. (p. 30), Cf. Naum Gabo: 'I am constantly demanding from myself and keep on calling to my friends, not to be satisfied with that gratifying arrangement of elemental shapes, colors and lines for the mere gratification of arrangement; I demand that they shall remain only means for conveying a well-organized and clearly defined image – not just some image, any image, but a new and constructive image by which I mean that which by its very existence as a plastic vision should provoke in us the forces and the desires to enhance life,

assert it and assist its further development.' 'On Constructive Realism', *Three Lectures on Modern Art*, New York (Philosophical Library), 1949, p. 83

22. (p. 30), For a demonstration of the significance of this fact, see Zuckerkandl, *op. cit.*, *passim*

II BEAUTY AND UGLINESS

1. (p. 33), Peter Selz, *New Images of Man*, New York (Museum of Art), 1959

2. (p. 35), Aristotle (*Poetics* V, i) describes the comic (τὸ γελοῖον) as a part (subdivision) of the ugly (τὸ αἰσχρόν). The comic mask, he says, 'is something ugly and misshapen without implying pain'.

3. (p. 35), My quotations are from the second edition, edited with an Introduction and Notes by J. T. Boulton, London (Routledge & Kegan Paul), 1958

4. (p. 36), Allen Tate, 'Longinus', *Lectures in Criticism*, New York (Bollingen Series), 1949, pp. 43-70. For the influence of Longinus on English criticism see T. R. Henn, *Longinus and English Criticism*, Cambridge, 1934

5. (p. 37), *Op. cit.*, p. 124

6. (p. 39), Cf. William Empson, *Seven Types of Ambiguity*, London (Chatto & Windus), 1931; Ernst Kris and Abraham Kaplan, 'Aesthetic Ambiguity', in *Psycho-analytical Explorations in Art*, New York (International Universities Press), 1952, ch. 10

7. (p. 40), Part I, section XIX, 'The Conclusion'

8. (p. 42), Vernon Lee, *The Beautiful* (Cambridge Univ. Press), 1913, p. 99

9. (p. 44), André Parrot, *Sumer*, Paris (Gallimard) and London

(Thames and Hudson), 1960, p. 106

10. (p. 45), *Op. cit.*, p. xxv

11. (p. 46), Cf. Janheinz Jahn, *Muntu; an Outline of Neo-African Culture*, trans. Marjorie Grene, London (Faber), 1961. Original edition Eugen-Diederichs-Verlag, 1958. Jahn bases this account of African philosophy on Alexis Kagame, *La philosophie banturwandaise de l'Etre*, Brussels, 1956

12. (p. 47), Eliot Elisofon and William Fagg, *The Sculpture of Africa*, London (Thames and Hudson), 1958

13. (p. 49), *Op. cit.*, Part Two, section V

14. (p. 50), Christian Zervos, 'Conversation avec Picasso' in *Cahiers d'Art*, Paris, 1935, vol. 10, no. 10, pp. 173-8

15. (p. 50), Statement in *Unit one*, edited by Herbert Read, London (Cassell), 1934

16. (p. 51), *Aeneid* VIII, 429-32:

Tres imbris torti radios, tres nubis aquosae
Addiderant; rutili tres ignis et alitis austri;
Fulgores nunc terrificos, sonitumque, metumque
Miscebant operi, flammisque sequacibus iras.

17. (p. 55), Cf. 'The Flower of Paece', *Eranos Jahrbuch* XXVII, 1959, p. 318

18. (p. 55), *Collected Works*, vol. 8, pp. 123-4

19. (p. 57), *The Archetypes of the Collective Unconscious. Collected Works*, vol. 9, part I, 237
20. (p. 58), Cf. *Aion*, III. *Collected Works*, vol. 9, part II
21. (p. 58), Cf. Melanie Klein, *Contributions to Psycho-analysis*, London (Hogarth Press), 1948, pp. 249, 269-70
22. (p. 58), *Beyond the Pleasure Principle*, Eng. trans. London (Hogarth Press), 1942, p. 66
23. (p. 60), *Op. cit.*, pp. 268-9
24. (p. 60), *Ibid.*, p. 268
25. (p. 60), 'Form in Art: A Psycho-analytical Interpretation', *J. of Aesthetics and Art Criticism*, vol. XVII, no. 2 (1959), p. 198
26. (p. 61), 'On the Nature of Ugliness and the Creative Impulse', *Int J. Psycho-analysis* XXI, part 3, 1940
27. (p. 61), 'A Psycho-analytical Approach to Aesthetic', *Int. J. Psycho-analysis* XXXIII, part II
28. (p. 63), *Abstraction and Empathy: a Contribution to the Psychology of Style*, trans. by Michael Bullock from the 11th German edition. London (Routledge & Kegan Paul), 1953
29. (p. 63), *Ibid.*, p. 45
30. (p. 63), In: *The Schools of Art in Florence* (1874)
31. (p. 65), *Op. cit.*, p. 212

III THE ORIGINS OF FORM IN THE PLASTIC ARTS

1. (p. 67), Kenneth P. Oakley, *Man the Tool-maker*, London (British Museum), 1958, pp. 2-3
2. (p. 67), The pioneer among chimpanzee painters was a female called Alpha, at the Yerkes Laboratory in the United States. An analytical study of her drawings was published by *The Journal of Comparative and Physiological Psychology*, vol. 44, 1951, pp. 101-11. For Dr Morris's analysis of Congo's painting, see *The New Scientist*, 14 August 1958
3. (p. 68), For a clear account of this technical development see Sir Francis H. S. Knowles, Bart., *Stone-Worker's Progress*, a Study of Stone Implements in the Pitt Rivers Museum. Oxford University Press, 1953
4. (p. 72), J. Gunnar Andersson, *Children of the Yellow Earth*, London, 1934, pp. 293, 318
5. (p. 72), Carl Hentze, *Les jades archaïques en Chine*, 'Artibus Asiae', 1929, no. 4 – Cf. also Joame Jenyns, *Chinese Archaic Jades in the British Museum*, London, 1951
6. (p. 73), *Prehistoric Pottery and Civilization in Egypt*, New York (Bollingen Series), 1947, pp. 24-5
7. (p. 73), *Ibid.*, p. 25
8. (p. 75), *Ibid.*, p. 55
9. (p. 76), E. H. Gombrich, *Art and Illusion*, New York and London, 1960
10. (p. 77), *Palaeolithic Art*, London (Faber & Faber), 1960, pp. 24-5
11. (p. 78), This process of the formalization of the female figure is illustrated still more clearly in the Cycladic representations in marble of the female figure; these date from the third millennium BC
12. (p. 79), *An Introduction to Metaphysics*, trans. Ralph Manheim, Yale University Press, 1959, p. 60
13. (p. 80), *Op. cit.*, p. 134
14. (p. 80), Philip Wheelwright, *Heraclitus*, Princeton, 1959, p. 19
15. (p. 80), *Ibid.*, p. 131
16. (p. 81), *Ibid.*, pp. 14-15
17. (p. 81), Thomas Langan, *The Meaning of Heidegger*, London (Routledge & Kegan Paul), 1959, p. 193

18. (p. 82), Wainwright, *op. cit.*, p. 159. It is better to avoid, in the present discussion, the distinction between *physis* and *idea*. *Idea*, according to Heidegger, 'is a determination of the stable in so far and only in so far as it encounters vision. But *physis* as emerging power is by the same token an appearing. Except that the appearing is ambiguous. Appearing means first: that which gathers itself, which brings-itself-to-stand in its togetherness and so stands. But second it means: that which, already standing-there, presents a front, a surface, offers an appearance to be looked at.' (*Op. cit.*, p. 180) The Greek word for what is offered in appearance, what confronts us, is *eidos*

19. (p. 83), Fung Yi-Lan, *Chinese Philosophy*, trans. Derk Bodde, Peiping and London, 1937, vol. I, pp. 396–7

20. (p. 84), Wang Pi (A.D. 226-249), the famous *I Ching* commentator, attributes their invention to the first of these mythical emperors, Fu Hsi

21. (p. 84), Cf. *Children of the Yellow Earth*, London, 1934, chaps. x, xii, xiii, xxi

22. (p. 84), *The I Ching or Book of Changes*. The Richard Wilhelm trans. rendered into English by Cary F. Baynes, 2 vols., London (Routledge & Kegan Paul), and New York (Bollingen Series), 1951

23. (p. 85), Charles W. Hendel, 'Introduction' to Ernst Cassirer, *The Philosophy of Symbolic Forms*, New Haven (Yale University Press), 1953, vol. I, p. 57

24. (p. 86), Ernst Cassirer, *Essay on Man*, New York (Doubleday Anchor Books), 1953, p. 182

25. (p. 86), *Essay*, p. 193

26. (p. 87), *Phil. of Symbolic Forms*, I, p. 106

IV INFORMALITY

1. (p. 89), New York University Press, New York, 1961. Subtitled 'A Phenomenological Inquiry'. Edited by H. W. Janson

2. (p. 89), New York (Bollingen Series) and London (Phaidon Press), 1960

3. (p. 89), Rudolf Arnheim in *The Art Bulletin*, vol. XLIV, no. 1, p. 79

4. (p. 90), *Op. cit.*, p. 4

5. (p. 90), *Ibid.*, pp. 24–5

6. (p. 90), *The Psycho-Analysis of Artistic Vision and Hearing*, London (Routledge & Kegan Paul), 1953. From this point onwards, the argument is based on a paper read by the author at the Fourth International Congress of Aesthetics, Amsterdam, August 1964

7. (p. 93), *Modern Painters*, vol. II, part III, sec. I, chap. V, p. 7

8. (p. 95), *The Eternal Present*, vol. I: S. Giedion, *The Beginnings of Art*, New York, Bollingen Series (Pantheon Books), 1962, p. 17

9. (p. 95), *Ibid.*, p. 22

10. (p. 95), *Ibid.*, p. 79

11. (p. 96), *Lascaux: Paintings and Engravings*, Harmondsworth (Penguin), 1959, p. 179

12. (p. 96), *Art and Scholasticism*, trans. J. F. Scanlon, London, 1930, p. 50

V FORM IN ARCHITECTURE

1. (p. 97), Professor Schapiro's essay is available in *Anthropology Today*, ed. A.L.Kroeber, Chicago (Univ. of Chicago Press), 1953, pp. 237-312. The use of the word 'form' in this definition is perhaps confusing: 'the constant element' would be a less ambiguous phrase from my point of view

2. (p. 98), New York (Bollingen Series), 1956

3. (p. 100), Cf. Werner Jaeger: *Paideia*, vol. I, p. 277. Oxford (Blackwell), 1939

4. (p. 100), *On the Nature and History of Architecture*. Trans. by various hands and privately printed by Victor Hammer at Lexington, Kentucky, 1954, p. 19

5. (p. 100), London (Duckworth), new edn., with Introduction by Herbert Read, 1932

6. (p. 102), *Ibid.*, pp. 38-9

7. (p. 102), *The Gothic Cathedral: Origins of Gothic Architecture and the Medieval Concept of Order*. By Otto von Simson. New York (Bollingen Series) and London (Routledge & Kegan Paul), 1956

8. (p. 103) *Form in Gothic*. London (Putnam), 1927, pp. 104-5

9. (p. 103), *Ibid.*, p. 105

10. (p. 103), *Op. cit.*, pp. 22-3. Von Simson uses almost identical phrases to describe Gothic architecture.

11. (p. 104), *The Sculpture of Gian Lorenzo Bernini*, by R.Wittkower. London (Phaidon Press), 1955, p. 32

12. (p. 106), *An Aesthetic Approach to Byzantine Art*, by P.A.Michelis. London (Batsford), 1955, p. 40

13. (p. 106), March Phillips, *op. cit.*, chap. V

14. (p. 106), Mies van der Rohe, 1923. Cf. Philip C.Johnson, *Mies van der Rohe*, New York (Museum of Modern Art), 2nd edn., 1953, p. 188

15. (p. 107), Johnson, *op. cit.*, p. 189

16. (p. 107), *Op. cit.*, pp. 12-13

17. (p. 108), From an appreciation written for the unpublished catalogue of the Frank Lloyd Wright Exhibition held at the Museum of Modern Art, New York, in 1940. Cf. Johnson, *op. cit.*, p. 201

18. (p. 109), *An Organic Architecture: the Architecture of Democracy*, London (Lund Humphries), 1939, pp. 10-11

19. (p. 110), *An Autobiography*, New York (1932) and London (Faber), 1945, pp. 484-5

20. (p. 110), *Op. cit.*, p. 50

21. (p. 111), *The Banquet Years: The Arts in France, 1885-1918*, New York (1955) and London (Faber), 1959, pp. 256-7

VI THE POET AND HIS MUSE

1. (p. 113), Cf. *The Forms of Things Unknown: Essays towards an Aesthetic Philosophy*, London (Faber) and New York (Horizon Press), 1960

2. (p. 114), An interpretation of the significance of Beatrice in Dante's life and work is given by Charles Williams, *The Figure of Beatrice*, London (Faber), 1943

3. (p. 115), *Ion*, 536b

4. (p. 116), *Ibid.*, 534b

5. (p. 116), *Ibid.*, 534d

6. (p. 120), *Poetry and Prose of William Blake*, ed. Geoffrey Keynes, London

(The Nonesuch Press), 1927, p. 1073

7. (p. 121), *Ion*, 534d

8. (p. 121), Preface to *Milton, op. cit.*, p. 464

9. (p. 121), Both poets were indebted to David Hartley (1705-57), whose *Observations on Man* (1749) has some claim to be considered as the foundation of associationist psychology. The Preface which Wordsworth wrote to the 'Lyrical Ballads' (1800) was also influenced by Hartley

10. (p. 122), *A Defence of Poetry* (1821)

11. (p. 125), *Essays* ('Characteristics'). I owe this reference to F. C. Prescott, *The Poetic Mind*, New York, 1922. (Re-issue, Cornell University Press, 1959, p. 97)

12. (p. 125), *Sigmund Freud: Life and Works*, London (Hogarth Press) 1953, vol. I, pp. 270-1

13. (p. 125), It has been assembled by L. L. Whyte in *The Unconscious before Freud*, New York, 1960; London, 1962

14. (p. 127), Collected Works in English, vol. 7, *The Art of Poetry*, New York (Bollingen Series), 1958, p. 319

15. (p. 127), *Ibid.*, pp. 315, 317

16. (p. 128), *Ibid.*, p. 20

17. (p. 128), *Ibid.*, p. 144

18. (p. 129), *Ibid.*, pp. 63-4

19. (p. 130), *Ibid.*, p. 61

20. (p. 130), *Ibid.*, p. 213

21. (p. 130), *Ibid.*, p. 214

22. (p. 131), Owen Barfield, *Poetic Diction: A Study in Meaning*, London (Faber & Gwyer) 1928, p. 244

23. (p. 132), I ignore the fact that many of our practical activities are habitual reflexes of which we can hardly be said to be 'conscious'.

24. (p. 133), Collected Works, vol. 7 (*Two Essays on Analytical Psychology*), New York (Bollingen Series), s. 274

25. (p. 133), *Ibid.*, s. 275

26. (p. 134), *Ibid.*, s. 374

27. (p. 134), *Ibid.*, s. 382

28. (p. 135), *Ibid.*, s. 387

29. (p. 136), *Ibid.*, s. 398

30. (p. 137), Sir Russell Brain, *The Nature of Experience*, London, 1959, p. 64

31. (p. 137), *Psychology*, London, 1892, p. 467

32. (p. 138), Cf. *Essai sur les données immédiates de la conscience*, Paris, 1911, pp. 10-14

33. (p. 138), Introduction by Hazel F. Barnes to *Being and Nothingness* (Methuen), London, 1957, pp. XIX-XX

34. (p. 138), Everett Knight, *The Objective Society*, London (Routledge & Kegan Paul), 1959

35. (p. 139), *Op. cit.*, p. 160

36. (p. 140), *Ibid.*, pp. 165-6

37. (p. 142), 'Dance and the Soul', trans. Dorothy Bussy (slightly modified). London, 1951. Quoted from Brain, *op. cit.*, p. 73. A more recent translation in Paul Valéry, *Dialogues*, trans. William McCausland Stewart. *Collected Works*, vol. 4. New York (Bollingen Series) and London (Routledge & Kegan Paul), 1957, p. 35

38. (p. 143), 'Problems in the Psychology of Art'. *Art: a Bryn Mawr Symposium*, Bryn Mawr, 1940, p. 272

39. (p. 143), *Jubiläumsausgabe*, vol. 39, p. 374

40. (p. 144), *Op. cit.*, p. 206. *The Principles of Art*, by R. G. Collingwood, Oxford, 1938

41. (p. 144), Cf. Collingwood, *ibid.*, p. 220: 'The condition of a corrupt consciousness is not only an example of untruth, it is an example of evil. The detailed tracing of particular evils to this source by psycho-analysts is one of the most remarkable and valuable lines of investigation initiated by modern science, bearing the same relation to the general principles of mental hygiene laid down by Spinoza that the detailed enquiries of relativistic physics bear to the project for a "universal science" of mathematical physics as laid down by Descartes.'

42. (p. 144), Collingwood, *op. cit.*, p. 207

43. (p. 145), Brain, *op. cit.*, p. 64

44. (p. 145), *Republic*, 382a-c: 'the falsehood in *words* is a copy of the affection in the soul, *an afterrising image of it . . .*' Trans. Paul Shorey

VII THE BIOLOGICAL SIGNIFICANCE OF ART

1. (p. 147), This story, entitled 'Schoolboys and Art', is translated by Aylmer Maude and included in *What is Art?* Oxford University Press, 1930, pp. 1-8

2. (p. 152), *Adventures of the Mind* (from the *Saturday Evening Post*). New York (Knopf), 1959, p. 10

3. (p. 154), 'Problems in the Psychology of Art', *Bryn Mawr Symposium on Art*, Bryn Mawr, 1940, pp. 260-1

4. (p. 155), *Gravity and Grace*, London (Routledge & Kegan Paul), 1952, p. 139

5. (p. 155), New York (Doubleday), 1959, p. 240

VIII HIGH NOON AND DARKEST NIGHT

1. (p. 161), *Meditations on Quixote* (1914), Eng. trans. by Evelyn Rugg and Diego Marin, New York (Norton), 1961, p. 84

2. (p. 162), *Ibid.*, p. 93

3. (p. 162), *Ibid.*, p. 99

4. (p. 163), Cf. J. F. Mora: *Ortega y Gasset*, new edn., Yale University Press, 1963, pp. 90-1

5. (p. 163), *Ibid.*, p. 30. Wilhelm Dilthey is another German social philosopher who was closely related to Ortega.

6. (p. 163), *Meditations on Quixote*, pp. 91-2

7. (p. 164), *Ibid.*, p. 99

8. (p. 166), Cf. Mora, *op. cit.*, p. 49

9. (p. 166), *Ibid.*, p. 63

10. (p. 166), *Meditations*, p. 96

11. (p. 166), *Ibid.*, p. 98

12. (p. 167), *Ibid.*, p. 100

13. (p. 167), I am excluding the consideration of ambiguity as a stylistic device, so ingeniously analysed by William Empson in his *Seven Types of Ambiguity*, though obviously such a device is characteristic of romantic rather than classic literature.

14. (p. 168), *The Art of the West in the Middle Ages*, trans. Donald King, London (Phaidon), 2 vols., 1963

15. (p. 168), *The Dehumanization of Art and Other Writings on Art and Culture*, Doubleday Anchor Books, n.d., p. 108

16. (p. 168), Cf. Otto von Simson, *The Gothic Cathedral*, New York (Bollingen Series), 1956, *passim*

17. (p. 169), *Man and Crisis*, trans. Mildred Adams, New York (Norton), 1958. The Spanish title of this volume is *El Torno a Galieo*, 1956

18. (p. 170), *Dehumanization*, p. 8

19. (p. 170), *Ibid.*, p. 10

20. (p. 171), *Ibid.*, p. 20

21. (p. 173), Philip Rieff: Introduction to Freud, *Genl. Psych. Theory.* New York (Collier Books), 1963, p. 10

22. (p. 173), Cf. *Man and Crisis*, p. 214

23. (p. 173), *Dehumanization*, p. 153

IX THE DISINTEGRATION OF FORM IN MODERN ART

1. (p. 179), Introduction to the catalogue of 'Painting and Sculpture of a Decade, 54/64' organized by the Calouste Gulbenkian Foundation. Tate Gallery, London, 22 April–28 June 1964

2. (p. 187), Cf. Martin Heidegger, *An Introduction to Metaphysics*, trans. Ralph Manheim, Yale University Press, 1959, *passim*

3. (p. 187), *Op. cit.*, p. 45

List of Illustrations

Index